BRANDING TYPOGRAPHY

ELEGANT/ RETRO/ HANDWRITTEN/ EXPERIMENTAL/ MINIMAL

GINGKO PRESS

Branding Typography

ISBN 978-1-58423-496-8

First published in the United States of America
by Gingko Press by arrangement with Sandu
Publishing Co., Ltd.

Text edited by Gingko Press.

Gingko Press, Inc.
1321 Fifth Street
Berkeley, CA 94710 USA
Tel: (510) 898 1195
Fax: (510) 898 1196
Email: books@gingkopress.com
www.gingkopress.com

Sponsored by Design 360°
– Concept and Design Magazine

Edited and produced by
Sandu Publishing Co., Ltd.

Book design, concepts & art direction by
Sandu Publishing Co., Ltd.

sandu.publishing@gmail.com
www.sandupublishing.com

Printed and bound in China

CONTENTS

TYPECAST

Creative Director
Figtree

MATT PARTIS

Which font to use? What style? Sans serif or serif? Upper or lower case? Minus or wide letter spacing? Hundreds of thousands of fonts are now available. How many no one knows, but there are many choices. What's more, these choices are now available to everyone. Anyone can be the typographer, the artist, the photographer, the web designer. Anyone can play the expert.

The public is becoming increasingly design and brand savvy and their aesthetic opinions can make or break a brand. Global corporations have been forced to backtrack on hugely expensive branding decisions just because members of the public didn't approve of their new typeface. The world of typography has become truly democratized and everyone has an opinion on it.

In a world of mass information with consumers constantly eager to learn more, there is additional pressure for typography to be more carefully considered and clearly support the vision of the brand.

Type is now loaded with associations. Just as brands have been conscious to adapt and become more relevant in the ways in which they communicate, the role of typography in branding has changed, too. The decisions surrounding typography have become more delicate, more complex and more significant. In some cases the typography can even carry the brand on its own. It can be the simplest way of explaining a brand's personality and attitude, reducing the role of the logo to a piece of type or even rendering it redundant.

It goes without saying that a brand's core assets have a very important part to play in communicating its message clearly. And because of the growing awareness of typography in the public consciousness, what may seem like a simple choice of one typeface over another can now completely change perceptions. A rounded typeface can feel friendly or childish, a bold typeface confident or loud, a light typeface refined or fragile.

Industries have even begun to reflect certain styles of typefaces, almost categorizing them by sector. Many traditional corporate companies have realized they need to be seen as more people-focused. This desire to be the consumer's friend rather than a faceless corporation has resulted in an influx of softer, more visually approachable typefaces in the world of big brands.

When it comes to designing for different industries, widening the letter spacing can suggest a more considered premium brand, while the light weights of helvetica neue and avant garde now carry strong associations with the cosmetic and fashion industries. This sector categorization of type can be used as an opportunity for a brand to stand out from the competition, where a brand can play against convention and express and stand out through an unexpected, unconventional choice of typeface.

A brand is much more than the typography used to build it, but at the same time, typography now conveys so much about a brand. Making the right choice about the typeface used can say more than the words themselves. Get it wrong and you confuse your market and even alienate potential customers. Get it right, and a typeface can carry your brand language in an extremely powerful way.

TYPOGRAPHY – THE TRANSLATOR OF A BRAND'S DNA

Creative Director
Coast

*Frédéric
Vanhorenbeke*

Typography, more than any other mediums for branding today, should translate the DNA of the brand in a clear and precise way. The messages conceived by companies, individuals and institutions are vectors of meaning, and subliminal messages are conveyed through the designer.

This is why no one can avoid typographic choices. This matter has always been an important aspect of visual communication: it is the source of understanding and at the intersection of meaning and symbol. Visual communication has to be clear, considering the bombardment with information we encounter every day. Fonts, color, and shape are the first signals that allow the reader to understand the message and to grasp its intensity. A font of a certain type may highlight a message in its most "cold" informative way, while another will guide information to a more abstract aesthetic or experimental meaning.

For brands, the font will primarily emphasize the message, but if the meaning of the message is also supported by the aesthetics of form - highlighting the brand values - then there's a double success. Typographic creation for brands is a key element for marketers: the typographer, when drawing the font, gives meaning to the shape inspired by the DNA of the brand.

At Coast, typographic design specific to each brand identity is an important part of each project. It enables originality and allows different services and products to stand out. The distinction must be made down to the first informative object: the letter. In many cases, we use fonts available on the market, but when we do have time (font development takes between two and six months), we create specific fonts. In a competitive market, a specific font can be an essential tool: it contributes to the innovation needs and personalization of the brand. And if the meaning and form are as one, faster brand awareness is gained. As for a logo, typography can reach this maximum function: symbolizing a brand by its form.

As the growth for simplification of messages follows the simplification of forms (take the example of simplified user friendly Apple computers between 2001 and 2011), the growth for brand attribution also increases. Communicating with the same typefaces may cause brand problems of attribution, if for example a competitor uses the same font family or a very similar one. Similarity in the brand world should be avoided. Similarity means weakness or plagiarism. Developing custom-made typefaces for brands is also a useful marketing tool: it keeps brands away from being seen as copycats or followers.

The 21st century is the century of information and typography is a vital method of information transmission.

ELEGANT

Some typefaces always convey elegance, sophistication, and style —
Futura, Caslon, Courier and Baskerville, among others. These can be
used alone or with ornamentation to emphasize a sense of luxury and
glamour for industries such as fashion and cosmetics.

'wich

'wich is the first concept sandwich shop in Hong Kong. It offers a unique variety of gourmet sandwiches to suit customers' varying tastes and appetites over the course of the day. Homemade soups, freshly prepared salads, delicate espresso drinks and fine wine by the glass are also served to complement the 'wich experience. The dishes are simply sumptuous works of art: a delight to customers' eyes and taste buds.

BLOW was asked to create the visual identity and packaging system for 'wich. To project the sophisticated image of a high quality gourmet sandwich, they have developed a visual identity with a cool color tone. Also, a series of ingredient icons were created to form the look & feel system. The master design was applied to all in-store collaterals, including the packaging system, in store collateral, uniforms for chef & waiters, as well as the signage system & environmental graphics, etc.

Client: 'wich Concept Limited
Design Agency: BLOW
Creative Direction: Ken Lo
Design: Ken Lo, Crystal Cheung, Caspar Lp
Illustration: Crystal Cheung
Photography: Brian Ching
Fonts in Use: Futura

ELEGANT

'wich

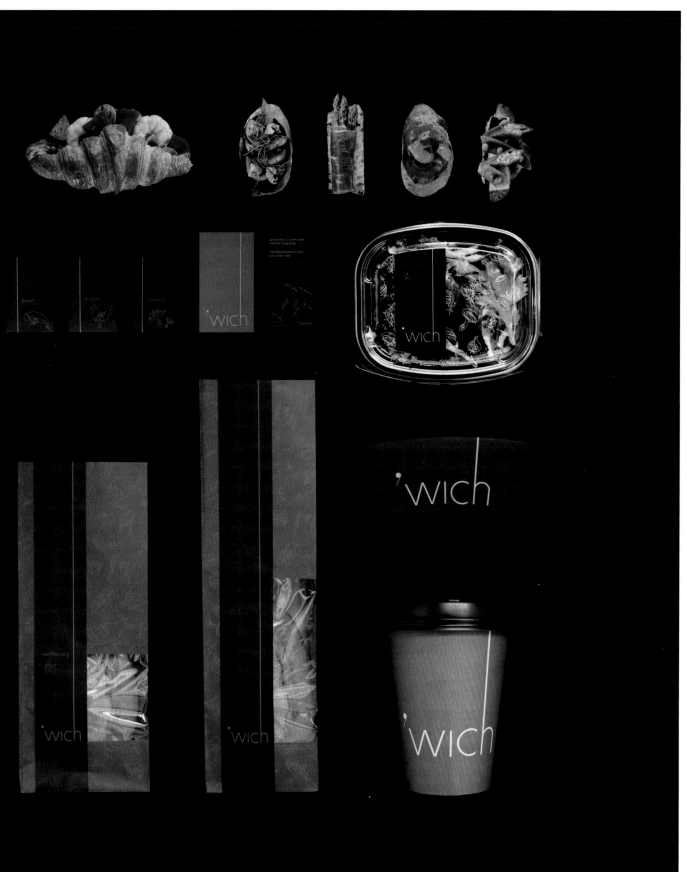

'wich

Davina Peace

Identity and packaging design for the London/ UK
based beauty brand.

Client: Davina Peace
Design Agency: Micha Weidmann Studio
Fonts in Use: Big Caslon

ELEGANT

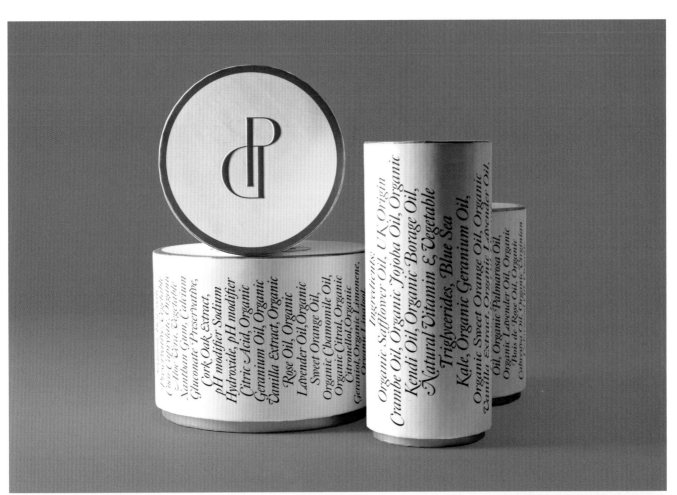

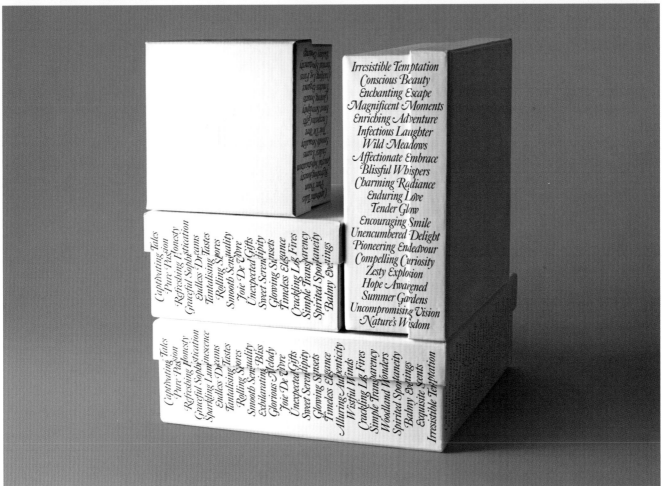

Davina Peace

Pedro Garcia
Identity

The new brand identity for Pedro Garcia shoes was based on the development of a graphic system created exclusively from the typeface Caslon 540. The texts are composed by using basic rules of implementation which creates a very distinctive personality. The typography applied in delicate black and white. The logo thus becomes a block of text that includes the full address and details of the company and shares the same rules as the rest of the information. The logo was implemented throughout the corporate typeface of the company computer system so that the composition of letters, texts, and bills always follow the same rules.

Client: Pedro Garcia
Design Agency: Clase bcn
Art Direction: Daniel Ayuso
Design: Daniel Ayuso, Malva García
Fonts in Use: Caslon 540

ELEGANT

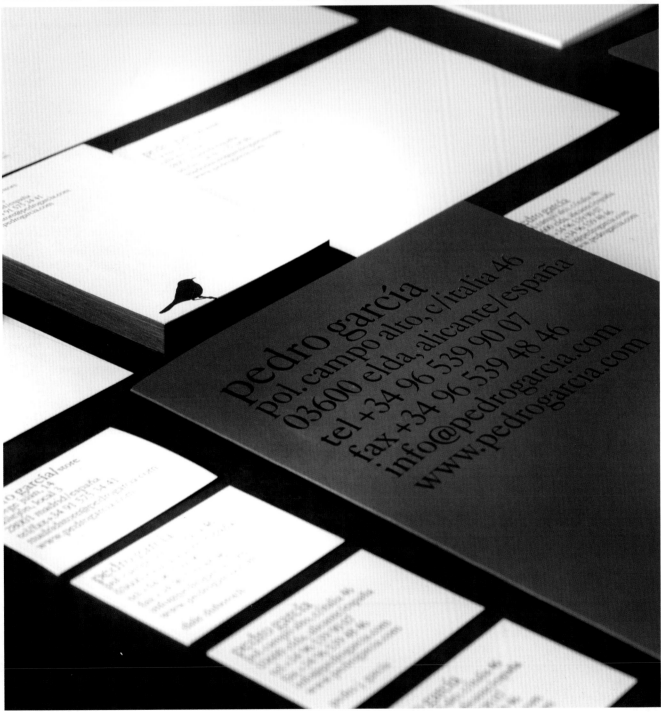

Pedro Garcia Identity

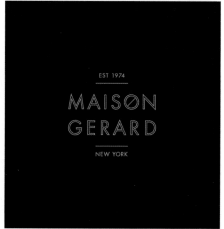

ELEGANT

Maison Gerard

Founded in 1974, Maison Gerard specializes in fine French Art Deco furniture, lighting and objects d'art. With a showroom and a new gallery both located on Manhattan's East 10th street, Maison Gerard offers a curated selection of classic and contemporary pieces for its high end customers.

Client: Maison Gerard
Design Agency: Mother Design
Creative Direction: Michael Ian Kaye
Design Direction: Christian Cervantes
Design: Christopher Rogers
Photography: Josh Dalsimer,
Robert Levin, Jason Levia
Fonts in Use: Futura/ Courier

Maison Gerard

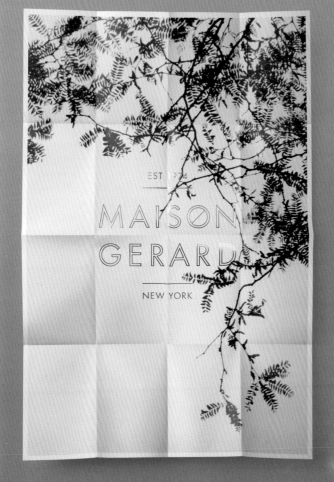

Maison Gerard

ELEGANT

Jackson Gilmour

Jackson Gilmour is a family run, chef-led and award-winning catering company. With a prestigious client list that includes HRH the Queen and a staff of chefs with more than a few Michelin stars between them, they needed a rebrand that conveyed their reputation as one of the best in the business.

Focusing on their unique identity as a chef-led catering firm, Magpie Studio devised a brand language reminiscent of cookery and recipes. Add a dollop of typography inspired by copper pot hallmarks, a twist of the diagrammatic language of family trees, and a tablespoon of very expensive print techniques, then heat at a high temperature and you end up with a chef-led, engaging and high-end rebrand.

Client: Jackson Gilmour
Design Agency: Magpie Studio
Creative Direction: David Azurdia,
Ben Christie, Jamie Ellul
Design: Jamie Ellul, Ben Atkins
Fonts in Use: ITC Johnston/ Serifa

Jackson Gilmour

ALPHA
MENS—WEAR
(SHOREDITCH)
LONDON
&
東京

ALPHALONDONDOTCOM

SELF/EDGE JAPANESE DENIM
by
EDWIN JEANS, LEE VINTAGE JEANS, BLUEBELL JEANS by
WRANGLER, STUDIO D'ARTISAN, ALLEVOL, TROUSERS
LONDON JEANS, DENHAM JEANS & CARHARTT JEANS.

ALPHA

Alpha London

The "Alpha" male concept runs through all branded communication. By using imagery of the North Alaskan timber wolf, BERG evoked a sense of danger and raw power. Combined with a strong color palette of red and black with minimalist typographic treatments, this resulted in a confident, sophisticated, provocative brand identity.

Client: Alpha Menswear
Design Agency: BERG
Design: Daniel Freytag @BERG
Photography: Daniel Freytag
Fonts in Use: Edelsans

ELEGANT

ALPHALONDONDOTCOM

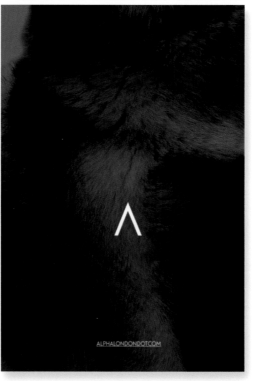

ALPHALONDONDOTCOM

Alpha London

ELEGANT

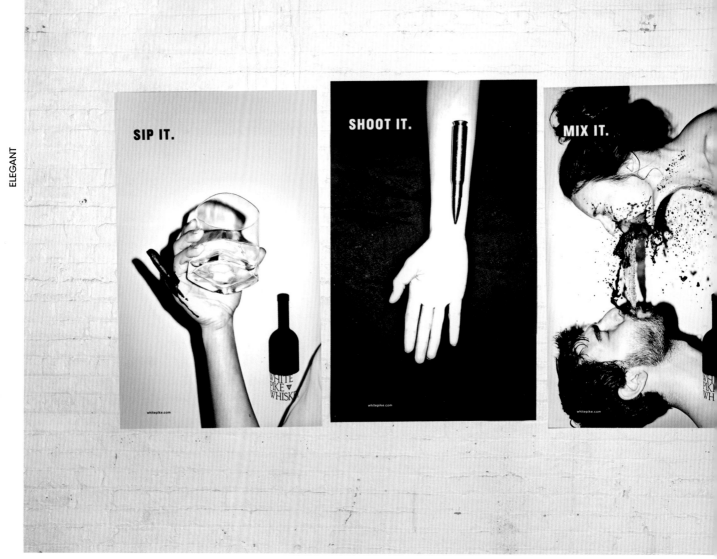

White Pike Whiskey

White Pike Whiskey

Crafted by a man trained in the Alabama school of fast whiskey, White Pike is a refined spirit made to be shot, sipped, or mixed. A recipe of corn, spelt and malted wheat, White Pike is distilled with precision for a smooth stand-alone flavor that mixes in ways brown whiskeys won't.

Highball, flask or straight from the bottle - drink it however and wherever. Not a single sounce of White Pike Whiskey has ever spent more than 18 minutes in prison.

Client: White Pike Whiskey
Design Agency: Mother Design
Creative Direction: Paul Malmstrom, Mark Aver, Blaise Cepis
Design: Peter Karras, Andew Lim, Mark Aver, Kapono Chung, Matt Wenger
Copywriting: Ben Hieger, Laura Perlongo, Peter Karras
Photography: Peter Karras, Blaise Cepis, Mark Aver, Jason Leiva
Fonts in Use: Custom type/ Akzidenz-Grotesk Buch/ Courier New/ ITC Cheltenham

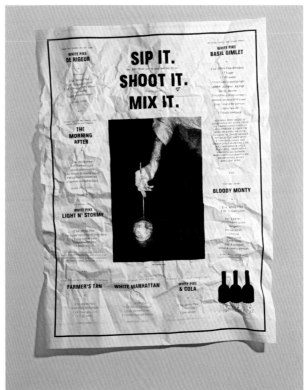

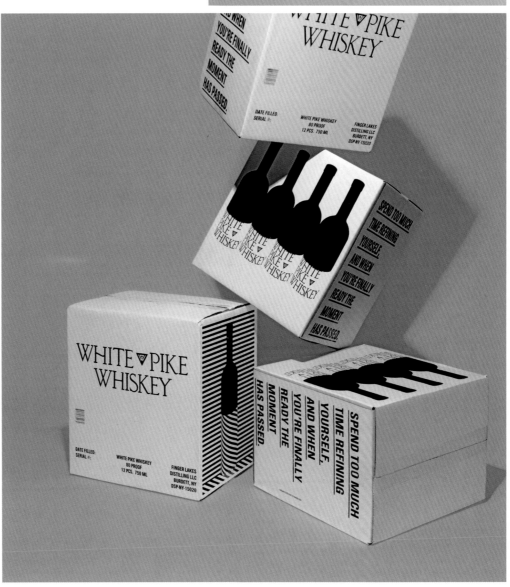

White Pike Whiskey

ELEGANT

freigaenger

freigaenger is a small fashion label that produces exclusive clothing. Raum Mannheim developed their corporate identity, including concepts for photography and advertising. They also designed posters, style-cards, a website for promotion, and a stand for the fashion fair "blickfang."

Client: freigaenger Fashion Label
Design Agency: Raum Mannheim
Design: Frank Hoffmann
Photography: OPM Fotografie
Fonts in Use: Base

freigaenger

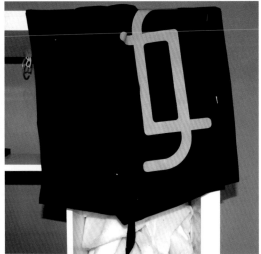

ELEGANT

Bespoke

Bespoke is a membership program run by Manhattan Loft Corporation as a way of thanking their residents. By collaborating with a number of handpicked elite, specialist companies, Bespoke was set up in 2009 to offer special deals and services to residents.

KentLyons were approached to create the identity, a micro-site and a limited edition membership card. The card was produced by screen printing flame-edge Perspex. Each one was then laser engraved with individual numbers and presented inside a metallic printed envelope.

Client: Manhattan Loft Corporation
Design Agency: KentLyons
Fonts in Use: Body text: Helvetica; Logotype: Hand-drawn and custom typeface for Bespoke

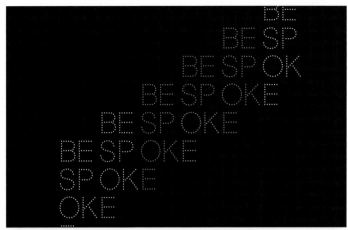

ELEGANT

Bespoke

Bespoke

Toscatti

Toscatti is a new brand of high endurance kitchenware. Their products are both very practical and long lasting. The client approached us to develop the brand's naming, identity and package design.

The brand currently has more than a dozen different containers, each with a different size and capacity. Anagrama developed a packaging system to categorize the containers in a practical manner. Each product's capacity comes first in the design hierarchy, and each product was matched with a distinctive color.

For the logotype they created a typeface with geometrical shapes, but with rounded strokes to give it a friendly feel.

Client: Toscatti
Design Agency: Anagrama
Architects: We Like Today
Photography: Caroga Photographer
Fonts in Use: Custom/ DIN

2.7 ᴼᶻ

15.6 ᴼᶻ

33.8 ᴼᶻ **toscatti.** ▪ airtight stainless steel container

57.5 ᴼᶻ **toscatti.** ▪ airtight stainless steel container.

2.7 ᴼᶻ

15.6 ᴼᶻ

33.8 ᴼᶻ **toscatti.** ▪ airtight stainless steel container.

57.5 ᴼᶻ **toscatti.** ▪ airtight stainless steel container.

Toscatti

ELEGANT

Acne Jeans Bauer

Acne Jeans Bauer

This rebrand for Swedish based Acne Jeans focuses on bold statements through the use of a stark black and white color palette, paired with bold typography.

Client: Self-Initiated
Design Agency: Kevin Cantrell Design
Design: Kevin Cantrell
Fonts in Use: Bodoni Bold Condensed

ELEGANT

Acne Jeans Bauer

ELEGANT

NIC–PATCH
Nicotine 21mg/24hour
7 Patches

HABTT

NIC-PATCH
21mg/24hour

Transdermal nicotine patch

As an aid to smoking cessaation
and for the relief of nicotine
withdrawl symptoms

Purpose
of use:

For smokers of 20 cigarettes
or more a day

For externel
use only.

Keep out of the reach of
children

Store under
25c°

Read enclosed leaflet
before use

Habit

Packaging design for Habit – a
company specializing in drug
rehabilitation and cessation products.
Habit believes in giving their
customers a luxurious, exclusive and
discreet experience through its wide
range of products. Treating addictions
ranging from nicotine to heroin, each
product is housed in a unique black
bottle or container to ensure your
rehabilitation will be completed in
style.

Client: Habit
Design: Morey Talmor
Fonts in Use: Futura/ A custom type
based on courier for the logo

Habit

Gallery LETA

Corporate and visual identity for
a gallery using cursive script. The
identity comprises the cursive
rendition of the gallery name with a
long end stroke that defines the logo
and forms a pattern that can be used
in various applications.

Client: Gallery LETA
Design Agency: Daikoku Design
Institute, the Nippon Design Center,
inc.
Design: Daigo Daikoku
Photography: Shun Takano
Fonts in Use: Bespoke

 ELEGANT

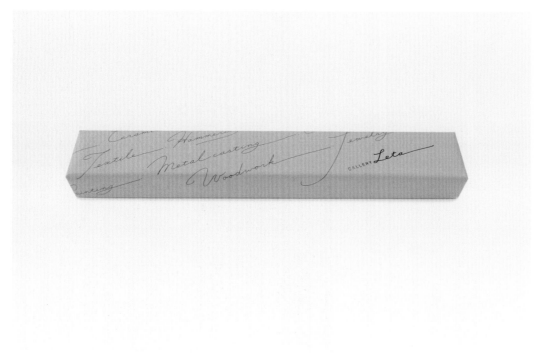

Gallery LETA

Gallery LETA

En Haute Joaillerie

Revitalized with an entirely new brand identity, luxury jewelers En Haute Joaillerie take on an expressive yet classic visualization of the qualities that a gift can bring. Explorations of the brand name "En", meaning "gratitude" in Chinese, spell out words with the "en" prefix; adorning the various packaging with a monochromatic cursive, lace-like typography, complementing the colored gems and jewels.

Client: En Haute Joaillerie
Design Agency: Asylum
Creative Direction: Chris Lee
Design Direction: Cara Ang
Design: May Chiang
Photography: Edwin Tan, Lumina Photography
Fonts in Use: Baskerville/ Customized fonts

ELEGANT

En Haute Joaillerie

En Haute Joaillerie

Sofia

Sofia

Sofia is a building designed by architect Cesar Pelli for One Development Group. Located in San Pedro, Mexico, this building was not only designed by an internationally renowned architect, but it also has the most generous specifications in every aspect: from automated appliances to Leed certifications.

Anagrama's task was to communicate such sophistication and exclusiveness to their potential buyers. Therefore they created an identity that was the exact opposite of what they usually see for this kind of project.

Sofia's identity is formed of three very important elements. The first is the logotype: the keys and the coat of arms are inspired by San Pedro's coat of arms.

For the typography, Anagrama developed a custom typeface designed especially for Sofia, which is inspired by British san serifs.

The layout of text and information is inspired by the typographical treatment used before grids were popularized by the Swiss grid system.

Client: Sofia
Design Agency: Anagrama
Photography: Caroga Photographer & Marco Más Chuy
Fonts in Use: Customized fonts

Sofia

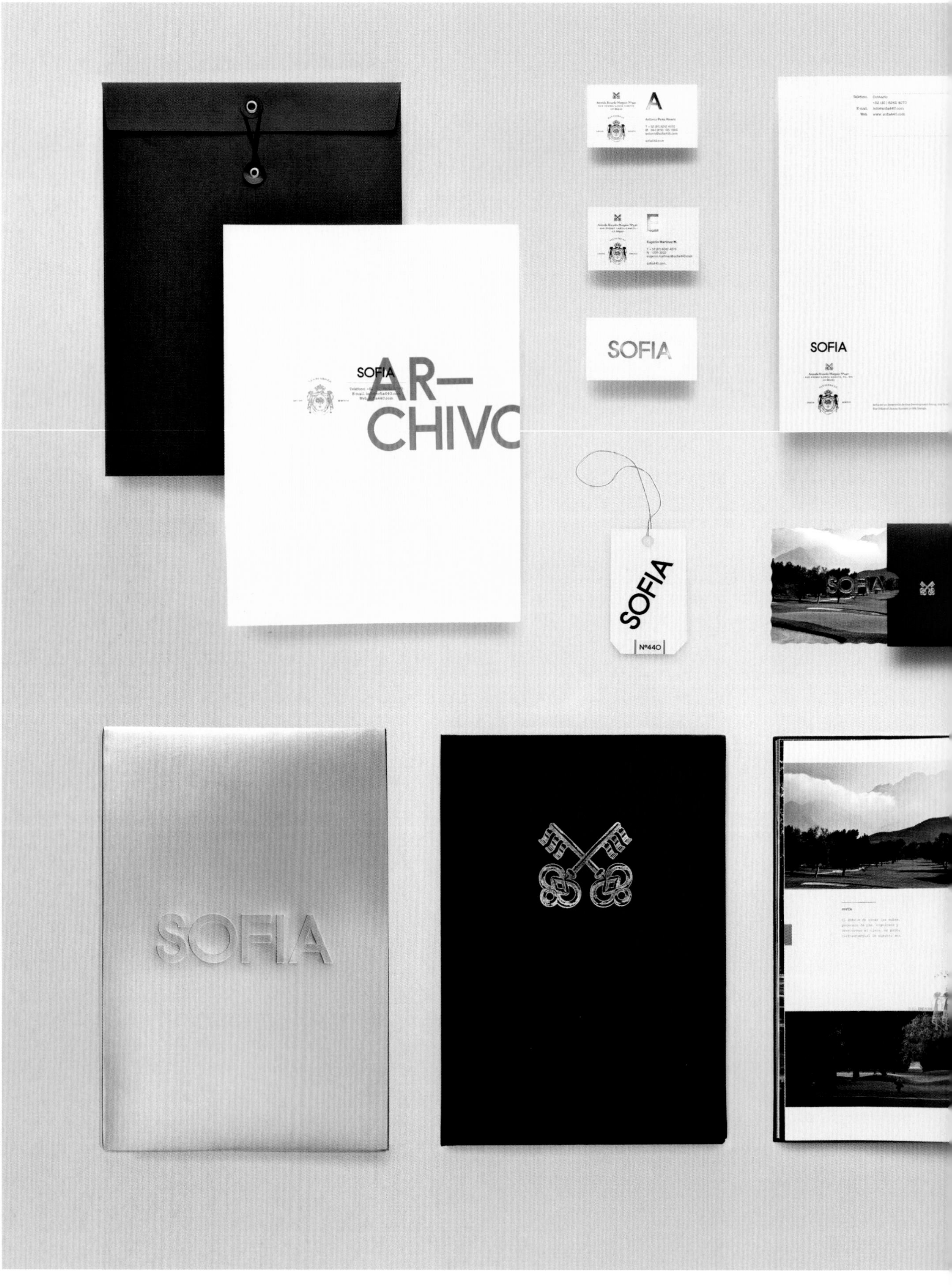

Sofia

Sofia

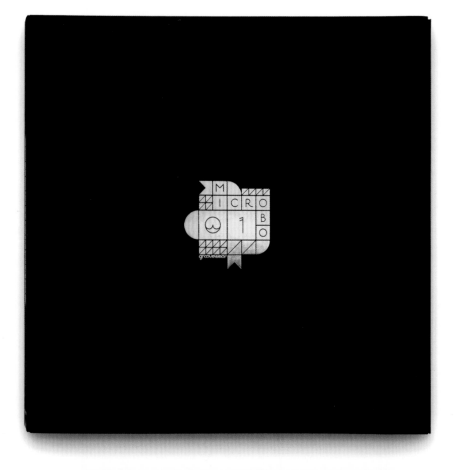

Groovewear

Starting from the logo designed by Emil Kozak, La Tigre worked on the identity, website and packaging for Groovewear. For the special limited edition boxes, they used fine papers, special printing techniques, and custom numbers.

Client: Groovewear
Design Agency: La Tigre
Fonts in Use: Estilo

ELEGANT

Groovewear

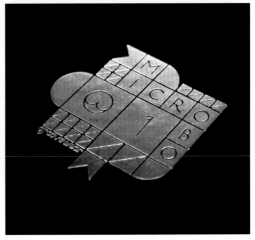

Groovewear

Queer Up North

With a proud 18 year history, Queer Up North has produced some of the most eye-catching and dynamic festivals featuring performances by an array of Gay and Lesbian artists. They wanted to show the whole world how different and exciting their festivals are.

The biggest challenge was to overcome stereotypes and reach out to not just a Gay and Lesbian audience but an audience who may not have considered attending a festival such as this.

By creating an array of identities and by "owning" the "Q," designer Matt Maurer was able to show how diverse this festival really is. By using a vibrant color palette of gold and black, the festival's uniqueness shines through.

Client: Queer Up North
Design Agency: True North
Design: Matt Maurer
Fonts in Use: Various typefaces

ELEGANT

Queer Up North

AIGA 100 Show Salt Lake City Chapter 2010

The AIGA 100 show 2010 identity plays off of the historic Utah road grid system. The identity is inspired by old Utah cartography. As an addition to this year's show, the coveted copper ingot returns to its original copper plate design.

Client: AIGA SLC Chapter
Design Agency: Kevin Cantrell Design
Design: Kevin Cantrell, Arlo Vance
Photography: Derek Israelsen Photography
Fonts in Use: Hoefler/ Various Ornaments

ELEGANT

AIGA 100 Show Salt Lake City Chapter 2010

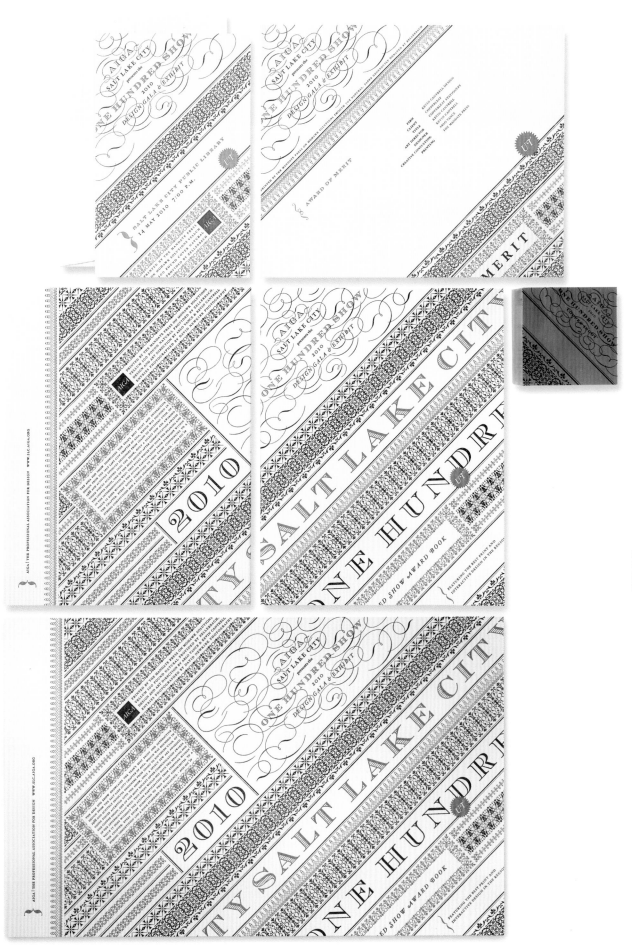

ELEGANT

AIGA 100 Show Salt Lake City Chapter 2010

Beta 5 Chocolates

The Beta 5 identity reflects the company's approach to the chocolate making process – a careful blend of science and craftsmanship. The packaging design was a carefully considered and executed method of brand development. Understated and refined, the packaging doesn't distract from the beauty and vibrancy of the products inside which are an exciting discovery.

Client: Beta 5
Design Agency: Glasfurd & Walker
Design: Phoebe Glasfurd
Fonts in Use: ArnhemFine/ GoodOT Book

Beta 5 Chocolates

ELEGANT

Beta 5 Chocolates

Ponshukan

Ponshukan

Ponshukan is a trading company that offers the best of Nigata: rice, food, and craftwork. The word Ponshu (本酒) is an abbreviated term of Nihonshu (日本酒). Kan (館) is defined as a warehouse. The first letter of po in the Japanese Katakana letter (ポ) and the Chinese character (本 - pon) are combined in the logo. The design incorporates the essence of the Nigata brand: elegance, hidden strength, authenticity, craftsmanship, and simplicity.

Client: Rakuichi Co., Ltd.
Design Agency: NIGN Company Limited
Design: Kenichiro Ohara
Fonts in Use: Bespoke

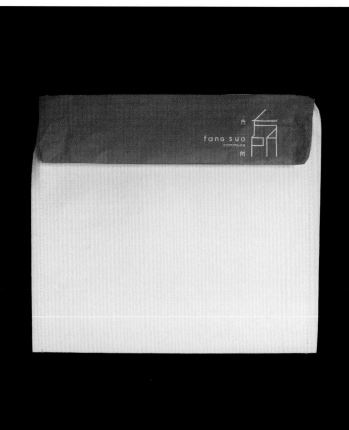

ELEGANT

Fang Suo Commune

Fang Suo Commune is not only a bookstore. It is an attitude, a statement, and an attempt to magnify the aesthetics of daily life. Fang Suo, a commune originates in Mainland China, became a platform for combining culture and aesthetics, a space that embraces rationality and sensibility, and a hybrid of knowledge, style and life. People can pursue truth and taste beauty here. New concepts, work, art, novels, poems, plays, music, and design can be found here.

Client: Fang Suo Commune
Design Agency: Mixmind Art & Design Co.,Ltd, Flâneur Co., Ltd., 84000 Communications Ltd
Strategy: Mao Jihong, Liao Meili
Design Direction: Stanley Wong
Design: Stanley Wong, Ye Min, Bethany Ho
Production: Huang Shang, Yang Tianmei
Fonts in Use: Bespoke

Fang Suo Commune

ELEGANT

Fang Suo Commune

ELEGANT

Kapok Identity

Kapok is a design retail store and café based in Hong Kong. The identity is inspired by the kapok tree which the brand is named after. Using the letter "k" as a modular unit, H55 created a visual identity that is well-crafted, organic and always growing to reflect the range of products which the store retails.

Client: Kapok, Hong Kong
Design Agency: H55
Creative Direction: Hanson Ho
Design: Hanson Ho
Fonts in Use: Bespoke/ Helvetica

Kapok Identity

Kapok Identity

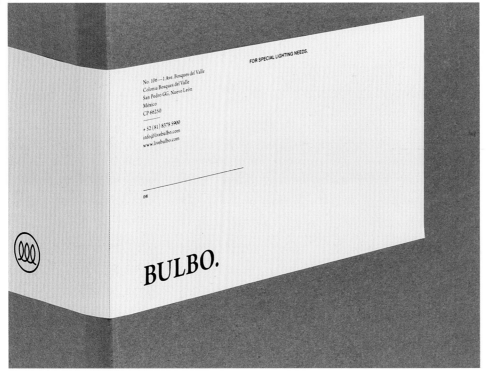

Bulbo.

Bulbo. is a lighting boutique specializing in premium points of purchase. Their added value relies on the fact that each of their pieces is carefully selected from their catalogue, as well as their ability to manage an entire lighting project for a specific space. When it came to their identity, Bulbo. knew the importance of portraying their products' sophistication. They approached Anagrama asking for a brand identity that communicated the brand's elegance above anything else. The monogram is inspired by the language of electric diagrams and it is complemented by a sober serif typeface.

Client: Bulbo.
Design Agency: Anagrama
Design: Sebastián Padilla,
Mike Herrera
Photography: Carlos Rodríguez
Fonts in Use: Arno/ HelveticaNeue
Bold

Bulbo.

Artemisia

Graphic identity and packaging concept for a range of smoking cessation products.

Client: Artemisia
Design Agency: Kurppa Hosk
Design: Thomas Kurppa

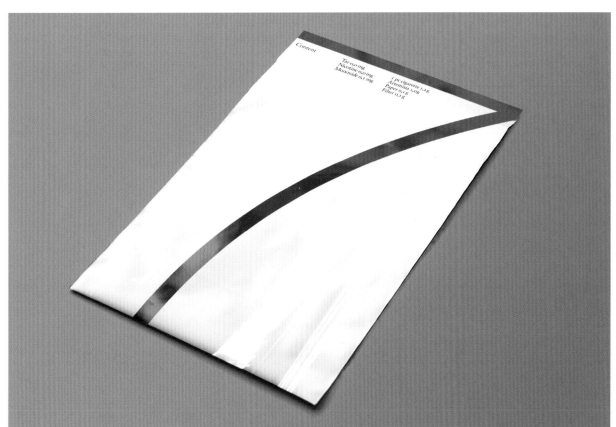

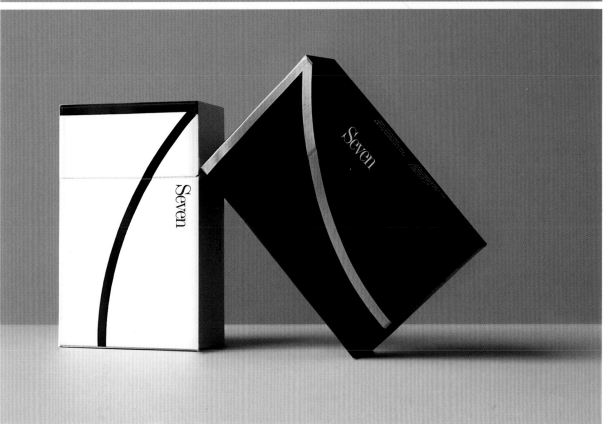

ELEGANT

Artemisia

RETRO

The prominent art and design movements between the roaring twenties and the early nineties still provide much inspiration for today's designers. Nostalgic typography, color usage, and illustrative elements highlight timeless aesthetics with handmade touches and twists of contemporary thinking.

Meat & Bread

The studio was approached to create a strong, masculine identity and brand design which communicates the restaurant's simple and uncomplicated offerings. The design had to be clean and minimal with a timeless appearance to the identity without feeling "retro". Strength through simplicity was the ultimate mandate.

Client: Meat & Bread
Design Agency: Glasfurd & Walker
Design: Phoebe Glasfurd
Fonts in Use: Knockout by Hoeer & Frere-Jones

RETRO

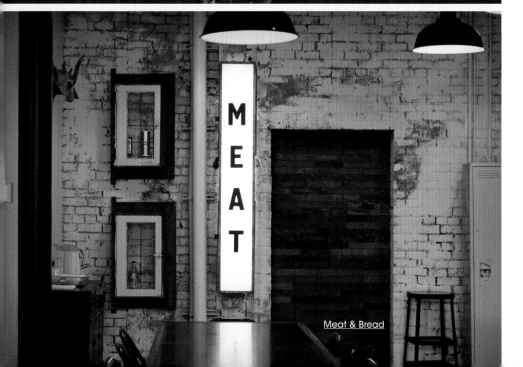

ORDER HERE

Meat & Bread

ArtFad

ArtFad offers prizes for contemporary art and artisanship, with the goal of stimulating research, creation, and excellence in the arts.

Client: a fad
Design Agency: Hey
Creative Direction: Veronica Fuerte
Design: Hey
Photography: Roc Canals
Fonts in Use: Futura

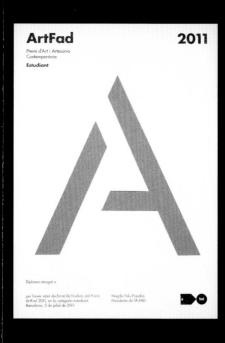

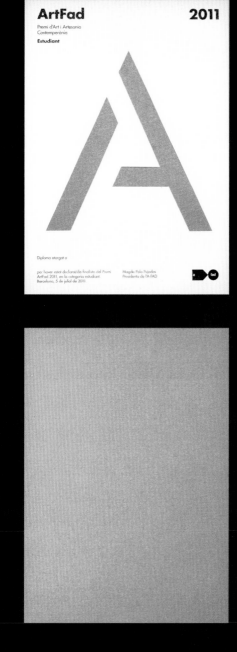

RETRO

ArtFad

1270 a vuit wine

1270 is a strong organic wine, produced by a small familiar cellar in the Priorat. To obtain a handmade feel for the packaging of the handmade wine, the label was produced manually, as if made by family members.

Client: Cellar Hidalgo Albert
Design Agency: Atipus
Fonts in Use: HTF-Bantamweight Champion/ Badhouse Light

RETRO

1270 a vuit wine

1270 a vuit wine

Wrap [rahyt] Takeaway

A concept of takeaway wrapping that breaks with the traditional look of the local pizzeria or shawarma bar in Denmark. [rahyt] is set in pronunciation brackets as it means several things: wrap right, wrap rite and wrap write. The project was an admission test for the Royal Danish Academy of Fine Arts School of Design.

Client: Self-Initiated (school project)
Design: Michael Hansen
Fonts in Use: Akzidens Grotesk

WRAP
[rahyt]
take away

Wrap [rahyt] Takeaway

AFTER ALL THE TROUBLE YOU GO TO

YOU GET ABOUT AS MUCH ACTUAL "FOOD" OUT OF EATING AN ARTICHOKE AS YOU WOULD FROM

LICKING 30 OR 40 POSTAGE STAMPS

RICE IS GREAT IF YOU'RE HUNGRY AND WANT 2000 OF SOMETHING

STEAK

MY FAVORITE ANIMAL IS

I WENT INTO A McDONALD'S YESTERDAY AND SAID 'I'D LIKE SOME FRIES.' THE GIRL AT THE COUNTER SAID 'WOULD YOU LIKE SOME FRIES WITH THAT?'

DO EAT ANIMAL CRACKERS

VEGETAR-RIANS

RED MEAT IS NOT BAD FOR YOU. NOW BLUE-GREEN MEAT, THAT'S BAD FOR YOU!

I'VE BEEN ON A DIET FOR TWO WEEKS AND ALL I'VE LOST IS TWO WEEKS

Coffee & Kitchen

The color world in black and white combined with brown determines the interior design as well as the corporate design of the Austrian daytime restaurant Coffee&Kitchen. moodley brand identity has consciously avoided corporate branding of the printed material, instead opting for a variety of logo stickers to convey the image of a relaxed and informal restaurant. The handwritten font intensifies this feeling even more.

Client: Coffeeandkitchen Gastronomie GmbH
Design Agency: moodley brand identity
Creative Direction: Mike Fuisz
Design: Nicole Lugitsch
Photography: Marion Luttenberger
Fonts in Use: Swiss 721/ Logo: Hand-lettering

Coffee & Kitchen

Coffee & Kitchen

Szelet

Szelet (which means "slice" in English) is a really small pizzeria which specializes in pizza by the slice. Kissmiklos started by inventing the name "Szelet". After that, kissmiklos designed its identity, interior design, packaging, and web design. The designer wanted the project to have a strong concept that could later be developed into a franchise, so a very intense shade of red was chosen. The familiar circular elements and style evoke the world of pizzeria and fast food restaurant.

Client: Szelet Pizzeria
Design Agency: kissmiklos (Miklos Kiss)
Fonts in Use: Birch Std./ Roboto/ Steelfish/ Caslon/ STIXGeneral/ Avant Garde Gothic/ Century Schoolbook/ Ostrich Sans/ Avenir Next/ Aachen/ Bebas Neue/ Bodoni Recut

RETRO

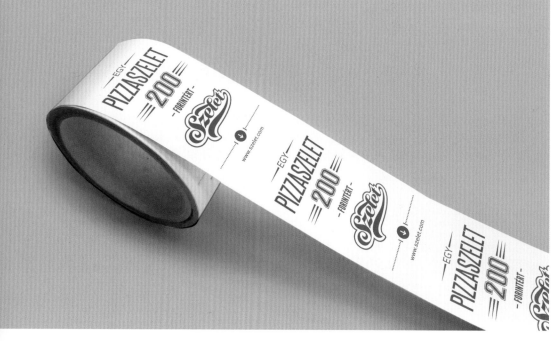

Szelet

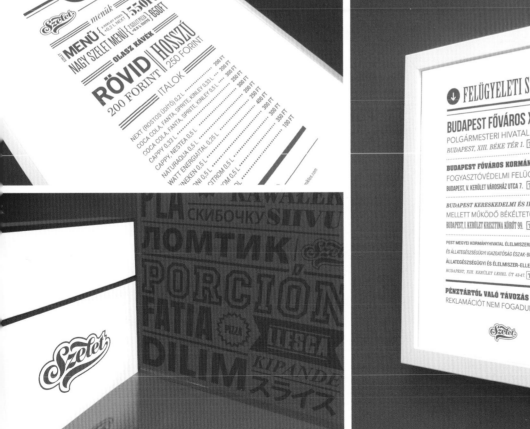

Szelet

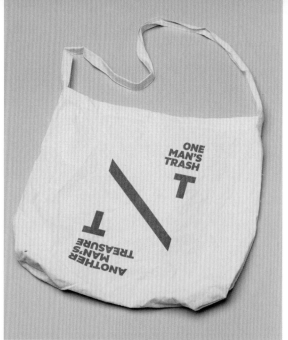

New Theatre

New Theatre is one of Sydney's oldest, proudest and most independent theatres. It is a people's theatre in the truest sense. Their ethos is about celebrating alternative theatre, offering unexpected twists, providing engaging experiences and helping to grow the careers of those involved. The logomark celebrates these unexpected twists and turns through the reveal of the "N" device, that stems from the word mark.

Client: New Theatre
Design Agency: Interbrand
Creative Direction: Mike Rigby
Design Direction: Christopher Doyle
Design: Eric Ng, Diana Chirilas
Strategy: Michelle Traylor, Gareth Stewart
Writing: Lex Courts
Fonts in Use: Metric

RETRO

New Theatre

New Theatre

Psaging®

Avui
pot ser
un gran
dia.

Psaging

Corporate identity for Natural Health & Beauty Nutrition stores.

Client: Psaging
Design Agency: Marnich Associates
Design: Wladimir Marnich, Griselda Martí, Anna Sodupe
Copywriting: Nenen Ruiz
Fonts in Use: Futura Maxi

RETRO

Natural Health & Beauty Nutrition

Yesterday
Today
Tomorrow

Psaging®

To be
or not
to be.

Psaging Friend

Lorena Pestana
Nutricionista

Psaging.

Life
is here
and
now.

Psaging.

Avui
pot ser
un gran
dia.

Psaging.

Good
aging
no
aging.

Psaging.

Haz
el humor
y no la
guerra.

Psaging.

RETRO

Psaging

RETRO

Hotel Daniel Vienna

Hotel Daniel Vienna embraces simplicity instead of flamboyant excess and fresh ideas instead of awkward hospitality. The hotel's owner, Florian Weitzer, calls it "Urban Stay/ Smart Luxury" – perfectly tailored to the needs of the modern traveler. This also applies to the design of the entire hotel, which is the polar opposite of heavy and sedate. It's designed in simple black and white with a personal touch.

Client: Weitzer Hotels BetriebsgesmbH
Design Agency: moodley brand identity
Creative Direction: Mike Fuisz
Design: Sabine Kernbichler
Photography: Marion Luttenberger
Fonts in Use: Trade Gothic Condensed/ Minion Pro/ Agenda Condensed

Hotel Daniel Vienna

Hotel Daniel Vienna

Hotel Daniel Vienna

PRIVATGRUND

BETRETEN ERLAUBT
FÜR FREUNDLICHE GÄSTE
DES DANIEL URBAN STAY

Zum Entspannen, Träumen und Genießen.

ES GELTEN UNSERE HAUSREGELN:

KEINE SCHLECHTE LAUNE   KEINE BETRIEBS-SPIONAGE   KEINE „HUNDE-GACKERL"   PARKEN VERBOTEN

RETRO

Hotel Daniel Vienna

ANIMA

Identity and posters for an animation festival in Brussels. This identity is a combination of computer animation and traditional animation. Hands have an important place in the design because in both computer and hand drawn pieces, they enact the first step of creation. Different techniques are used to complete the identity which defines ANIMA.

Client: ANIMA (personal proposition)
Design: Amélie Wagner
Fonts in Use: Handwriting/ Typ1451

RETRO

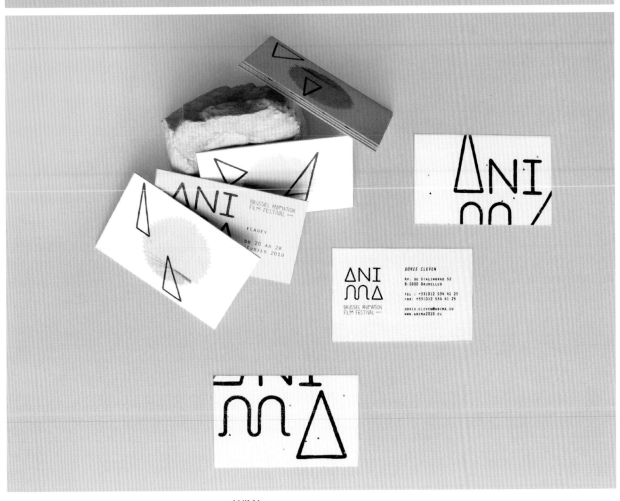

ANIMA

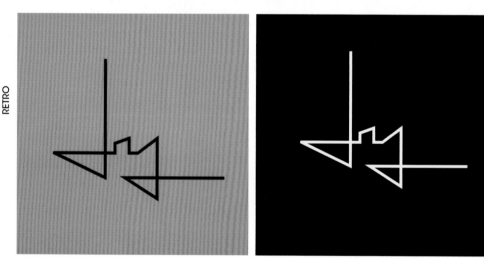

Life Needs Graphics

Life Needs Graphics is a motion graphics studio. As most of the material they present is in CD, DVD or blue-ray format, the design of the entire stationery line revolves around that.

Client: Life Needs Graphics
Design Agency: Manifiesto Futura
Fonts in Use: Numberplate Belgium

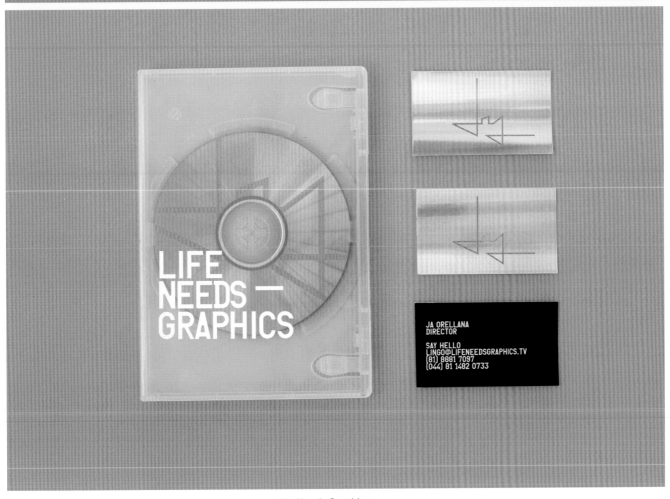

Life Needs Graphics

MORE Bike Park Identity

Responding to high-speed downhill bicycle sports as the main theme, FEB Design suggested an identity born from the direct synergy between illustration and typography (MORE Blackletter is a custom made type).

Using illustration enhanced the story-telling capability of the brand, enabling exploration of primary instinct images as stimulant entertainment (courage, fearlessness...), in order to establish an emotional bridge with the end user.

By delivering a flyer that can be transformed into a stencil, FEB Design maximized the user's interaction and increased its lifespan, making this expanded experience more memorable overall. After reading the flyer you can reuse it as a stencil and help spread the message.

The MORE Bike Park identity was designed in collaboration with the illustrator Pedro Lourenço.

Client: MORE Bike Park
Design Agency: FEB Design, FIBA Design
Design: Marta Fragata, Miguel Batista
Illustration: Pedro Lourenço
Fonts in Use: Bespoke MORE
Blackletter by FEB Design

MORE Bike Park Identity

MORE Bike Park Identity

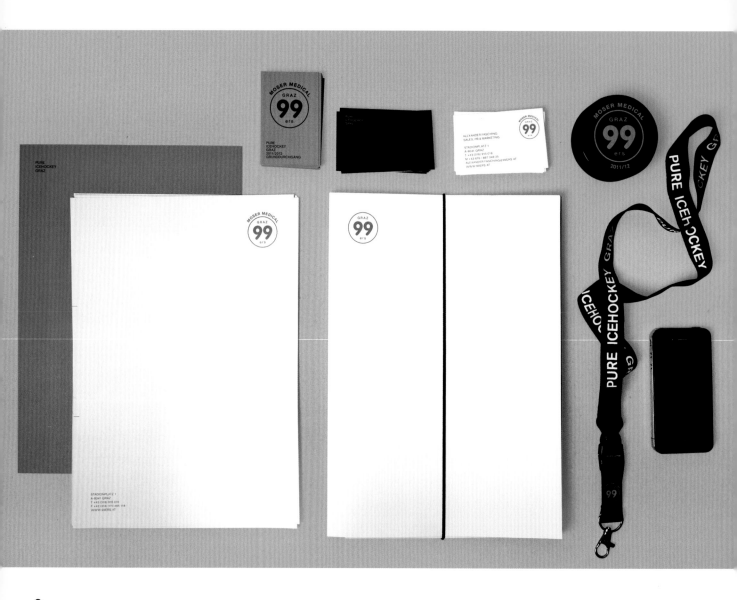

Graz 99ers

During the redesign of the Austrian ice hockey team "Graz 99ers", the aim was to concentrate on only the most important aspects. The result was: a straightforward logo, 2 colors, no coat-of-arms, no sentimentalities, only "Pure" Ice Hockey!

Client: Moser Medical Graz 99ers
Design Agency: moodley brand identity
Creative Direction: Mike Fuisz
Design: Wolfgang Niederl
Photography: Marion Luttenberger
Fonts in Use: Berthold Akzidenz Grotesk

Graz 99ers

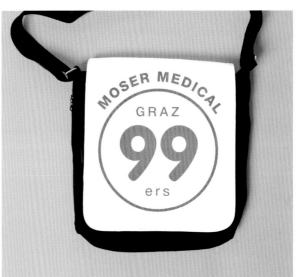

Graz 99ers

BLANC KARA

BLANC KARA
BOUTIQUE HOTEL SOUTH BEACH

205 COLLINS AVENUE MIAMI BEACH FL 33139 USA
INFO@BLANCKARA.COM
BLANCKARA.COM

T : 786 216 7205
F : 786 216 7005

BLANC KARA
BOUTIQUE HOTEL, SOUTH BEACH

205 COLLINS AVENUE MIAMI BEACH FL 33139 USA   T : 786 216 7205
INFO@BLANCKARA.COM   BLANCKARA.COM   F : 786 216 7005

BLANC KARA

BLANC KARA   205 COLLINS AVENUE MIAMI BEACH FL 33139 USA
BOUTIQUE HOTEL SOUTH BEACH   INFO@BLANCKARA.COM   BLANCKARA.COM

Blanc Kara

Identity and communication development for a new boutique hotel in Miami, Florida. In 2010, Coast was approached by a group of investors who wanted to open a brand new chain of hotels with a difference. Its name is Blanc Kara and its inspiration is "Art de Vivre à la Française" with the aim of creating a nest on the American market. A nest of tranquility and art, a nest for international travelers, culture freaks and art lovers. The Coast team worked on this on all levels, from brand pillars to all design output, creating a global experience. They took part in the development of specific communication idea, among them the creation of an original soundtrack by French band "Nouvelle Vague" to be sold in concept stores worldwide, and the development of an original magazine.

Client: Blanc Kara Boutique Hotel South Beach
Design Agency: Coast
Creative Direction:
Frédéric Vanhorenbeke
Design: Coast team
Photography: Serge Leblon
Interior Architecture: Delacroix & Friant associates
Fonts in Use: Blanc Kara typeface

Blanc Kara

RETRO

Blanc Kara

Deli

Graphic identity for Deli – an old school American style sandwich shop with a backdoor leading to a suave cocktail bar and mini club, located in Tel Aviv, Israel. The graphic language is a simplistic contemporary take on a traditional 1950s and 60s American diner aesthetic.

Client: Deli
Design: Morey Talmor
Fonts in Use: Futura/ Aduma

RETRO

Deli

Deli

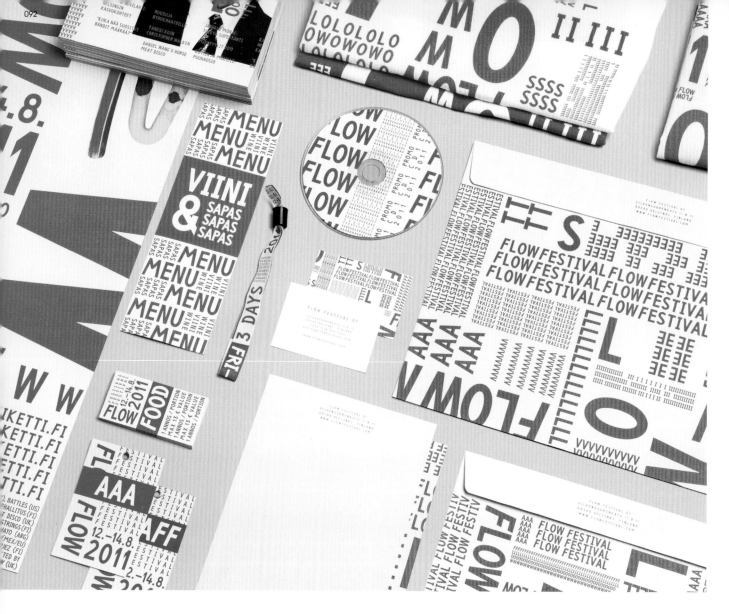

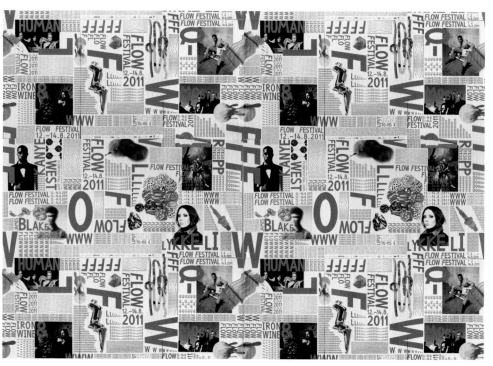

Flow Festival

The identity for Flow Festival builds on the idea of the festival crowd as an urban tribe, united by a metaphorical mantra of visual wordplay. The bespoke Flow-typeface is influenced by the contemporary central European trend of postmodern craftsmanship. Tsto sees the font as smart, easy to approach and with a sense of humor. Together with the illustrations by Santtu Mustonen, the repetition of letters and images creates the core visual language and imagery for the project.

Client: Flow Festival
Design Agency: Tsto
Illustration: Santtu Mustonen
Website: Byroo
Fonts in Use: Bespoke

Flow Festival

Flow Festival

MONU

MONU, short for "monumental", is the name of a spacious private venue located within a downtown retail and residential development. &Larry was asked to revamp the logo so as to better convey an epic three-dimensional sculpture like the venue's name evokes.

Up close, the letterforms are seen to contain a subtle paint spatter pattern which alludes to the creative possibilities that the space affords. Upon seeing photos of the actual space, one will also note the distinctive black columns that are reflected in the new brand mark.

The brochure itself is a play on spatial qualities, as it unfolds like a huge poster to reveal details and images of the venue to prospective customers.

Client: WOHA
Design Agency: &Larry
Creative Direction: Larry Peh
Design: Adora Tan
Copywriting: Kelvin Pang
Fonts in Use: Bespoke/ Akizdenz-Grotesk Condensed/ Univers

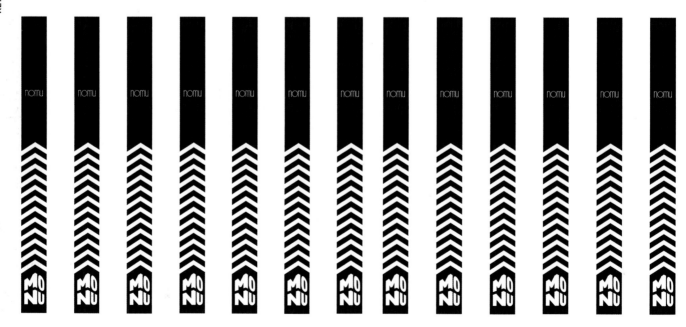

SPATIAL CANVAS, SPECIAL EVENTS.

AT 20 HANDY ROAD SITS A STRIKINGLY DESIGNED BUILDING BY AWARD-WINNING ARCHITECTS WOHA; WITHIN IT IS A SPACE AWAITING YOUR DISCOVERY AND PURPOSE: MONU.

LARGER THAN LIFE YET COMFORTABLY INTIMATE, MONU IS A MODERN AND VERSATILE VENUE THAT AFFORDS YOU THE FLEXIBILITY TO HOST EVENTS OF EVERY MAGNITUDE AND SOPHISTICATION IN STYLE.

IS LOCATED AT 20 HANDY ROAD 3RD FLOOR SINGAPORE 229236 WWW. MONU.SG

RETRO

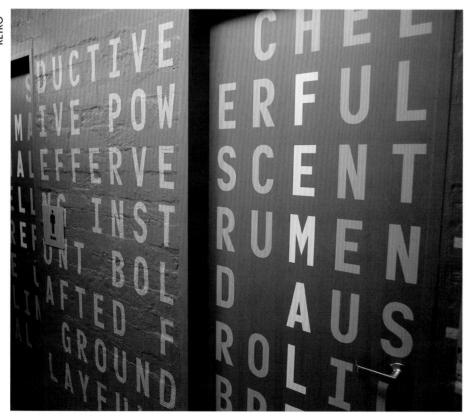

Griffin Theatre Company

Griffin Theatre Company is a "new writing" theatre at the forefront of Australian playwriting.

For the past 30 years, Griffin has brought together the country's most talented people to make some of Australia's most groundbreaking theatre. Since writing is at the heart of Griffin, the identity puts words centre stage. A simple crossword device threads the word "Griffin" or production titles through a list of words relevant to the play.

The mood can change from one production to the next by using different combinations of words, color and imagery to strike their own chord, while the backbeat remains distinctively Griffin.

Client: Griffin Theatre Company
Design Agency: Interbrand
Creative Direction: Chris Maclean
Design Direction: Andrew Droog
Design: Joao Peres
Fonts in Use: Monofonto

Griffin Theatre Company

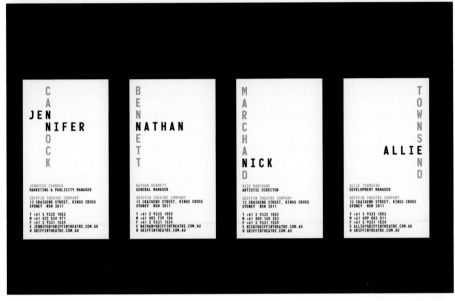

Griffin Theatre Company

SMETS

Identity development and signage system for a luxury concept store of 3,500 sqm of fashion, design and beauty items. The identity system Coast has created is made of the Smets typeface and icons, specially designed for the store. The signage system (on 4 levels) is made of laser cut plastic letters, mounted directly on concrete walls. Bright and colorful paints have been used for the parking spaces, bringing the shop experience to that level too. Within its walls, the Bowery restaurant sits above a Wine Bar and the S BAR. The Bowery restaurant sign is made in strong walnut wood, with oversized engraved logotype. For the S BAR, an optical 3D glass sculpture was made of vinyl, ensuring discretion and light. Coast has developed all identity appearances for the brand (corporate identity, signage, packaging, communication media, cards, and website).

Client: Smets Concept Store Brussels
Design Agency: Coast
Creative Direction:
Frédéric Vanhorenbeke
Design: Delphine Platteeuw
Architecture: Zoom Architecture
Fonts in Use: Smets typeface

RETRO

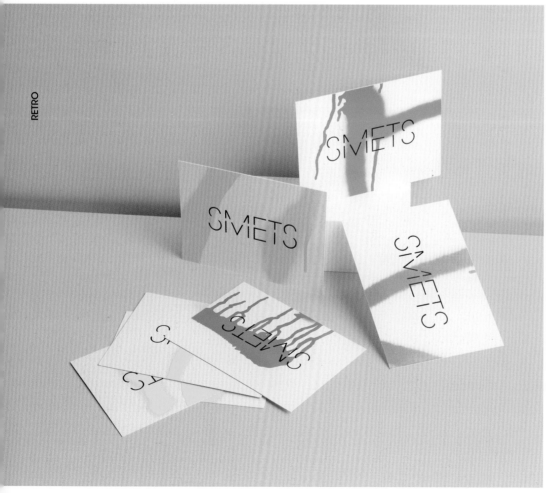

SMETS

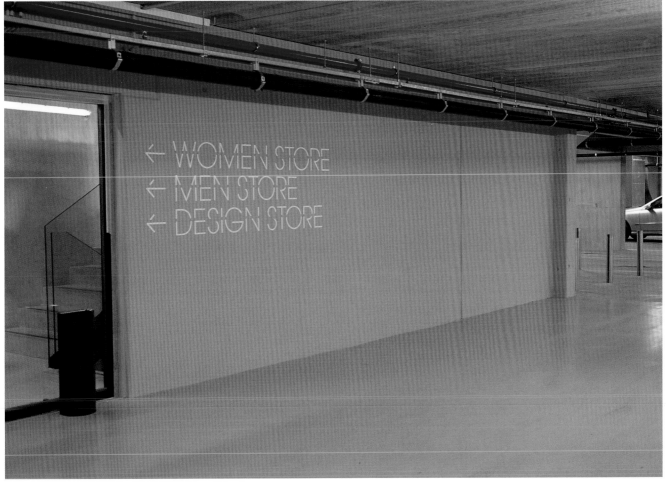

SMETS

Hemtex

Hemtex is the biggest Nordic retailer for home interior decoration. In order to reach a younger audience, SDL revitalized the brand identity including a unique font and numbers. Their inspiration was the rich Swedish textile heritage. As a result the brand awareness has increased and the company has shifted from loss to profit.

Client: Hemtex
Design Agency: Stockholm Design Lab
Creative Direction: Björn Kusoffsky
Art Direction: Per Carlsson
Design: Stockholm Design Lab
Photography: Philip Karlberg, Felix Odell
Project Partner: TEA
Fonts in Use: HEMTEX Alphabet

RETRO

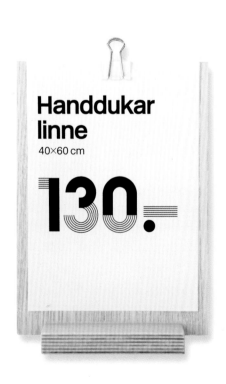

Handdukar
linne
40×60 cm

130.-

Hemtex

Waldo Trommler Paints

In 2011 Reynolds and Reyner finished two
projects redesigning the international paint
brand Waldo Trommler Paints. WTP is the most
friendly and remarkable brand of paints on the
shelf now. WTP has no corporate colors – it has
the corporate identity, common for each design
element – from business cards to packaging.
Every item has a bright and memorable
combination of colors and objects that together
form the entire brand. The paint proves for itself
that it is as high quality as its outer packaging.

Client: Waldo Trommler Paints
Design Agency: Reynolds and Reyner
Creative Direction: Artyom Kulik, Alexander
Andreyev
Font in Use: Bebas

Waldo Trommler Paints

TAKE
YOUR
PLEASURES
SERIOUSLY.

ART IS
NOT
WHAT
YOU SEE

WALDO
TROMMLER
PAINTS

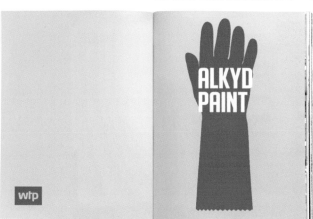

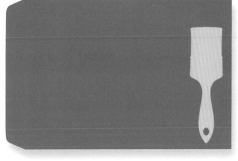

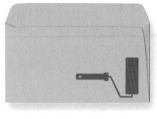

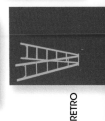

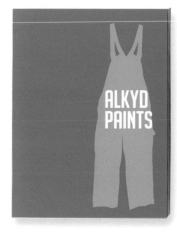

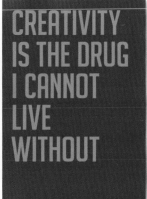

RETRO

Ajandék Terminál

Ajándék Terminál exhibition, fair and auction was one of the Christmas events organized by Design Terminál for Hungarian designers to showcase their work. Between the 9th and 18th of December, products from 50 talented designers could be bought. Design Terminál is a state owned, non-profit organization with its main goals the promotion of Hungarian design and culture, the organization of cultural events, and the exhibition of various international and Hungarian design projects for the public. kissmiklos was in charge of the graphic design and the image of the Ajándék Terminál, who combined the classical but new calligraphy with a vintage typographic elements.

Client: Design Terminál
Design Agency: kissmiklos (Miklos Kiss)
Fonts in Use: Serifa/ Franklin Gothic/ League Gothic/ Steelfish/ Times/ Old Standard/ Aachen/ Ogilvy Poster/ Helvetica Neue

VÁSÁROLJ DESIGNT KARÁCSONYRA! / BUY DESIGN FOR CHRISTMAS!

KARÁCSONYI DESIGN KIÁLLÍTÁS VÁSÁR AUKCIÓ | DEC 9–18 | CHRISTMAS DESIGN EXHIBITION FAIR AUCTION | DESIGN TERMINÁL | 1051 BUDAPEST ERZSÉBET TÉR 13

Kedves ....

Engedje meg, hogy ezúton szeretettel meghívjuk Önt és kísérőjét az Ajándék Terminál - karácsonyi design kiállítás és vásár - exkluzív árverésére, melyen magyar designerek által felajánlott egyedi tárgyakra lehet licitálni. A bevétel 10 százalékát jótékonysági célra fordítjuk, az összegből vásárolt rajzeszközökkel a nevelőotthonokat és az otthonukban nevelkedő gyerekeket ajándékozzuk meg. Az aukciót Winkler Nóra vezeti. ★★★★★★★★★★★★★★★

A Design Terminál december 9. és 18. között megrendezésre kerülő karácsonyi kiállítása és vására közel ötven magyar tervező munkáját mutatja be: a földszinten a legjobb magyar design tárgyak láthatóak, az emelet pedig különlegesen kialakított, elegáns divatüzletté alakul, ahol hazai divattervezők ruhái és kiegészítői kapnak helyet.

AZ ESEMÉNY IDŐPONTJA:

2011 DECEMBER 17 SZOMBAT, 18:00

MEGJELENÉSÉRE FELTÉTLENÜL SZÁMÍTUNK!

A DESIGN TERMINÁL CSAPATA

WWW.DESIGNTERMINAL.HU / 061 327 7205

Budapest 1054. Erzsébet tér 13. (a volt buszpályaudvar épülete)

AZ ESEMÉNYEN VALÓ RÉSZVÉTELRŐL VISSZAJELZÉST KÉRÜNK
A DESIGN@DESIGNTERMINAL.HU E-MAIL CÍMEN.

01 KARÁCSONYI DESIGN KIÁLLÍTÁS VÁSÁR AUKCIÓ CHRISTMAS DESIGN EXHIBITION FAIR AUCTION DEC 9 –18 DESIGN TERMINÁL 1051 BUDAPEST ERZSÉBET TÉR 13

01 KARÁCSONYI DESIGN KIÁLLÍTÁS VÁSÁR AUKCIÓ CHRISTMAS DESIGN EXHIBITION FAIR AUCTION DEC 9 –18 DESIGN TERMINÁL 1051 BUDAPEST ERZSÉBET TÉR 13

Aukció

Design Terminál

A DESIGN SZAKMA ÉS A DESIGN IRÁNT ÉRDEKLŐDŐK ÉLETTELI, PEZSGŐ KULTURÁLIS KÖZPONTJA A VÁROS LEGFREKVENTÁLTABB PONTJÁN, NYIRI ISTVÁN BAUHAUS ÉS SZOCIALISTA-REALISTA VONÁSOKAT MAGÁN VISELŐ ÉPÜLETÉBEN.

2011 DEC 17 18 ÓRA

AJÁNDÉK TERMINÁL

A Design Terminál 2011. december 9. és 18. közötti arculatot vált, és Ajándék Terminállá változik. Az ötvenkettő a bútortervezőktől kötél 50 tehetséges magyar tervező több szer tárgyaít állítja ki a kiállítótérben, és természetesen minden darab megvásárolható.

AZ AJÁNDÉK TERMINÁL DESIGN AUKCIÓJA

AZ AUKCIÓT VEZETI: WINKLER NÓRA.

December 17 én 18 órakor design aukciót rendezünk, ahol az Ajándék Terminállban kiállító designerek egyedi, kifejezetten erre az alkalomra készített tárgyaít lehet árverés útján megvásárolni. A bevétel 10 százaléka jótékony célt szolgál, s Design Terminál sajponzorok segítségével nevelőotthonokban élő gyerekeknek vásárol rajzeszközöket.

Az ajándékokat december 21-én 10 órakor, a Fikműhely által tartott foglalkozás keretén belül adjuk át a gyerekeknek itt, a Terminálban.

DEC 9 – 18

NYITVA HÉTFŐTŐL VASÁRNAPIG
12.00 ÉS 21.00 KÖZÖTT

DEC — 9. 18.00 A TOPLISTA STÍLUS MAGAZIN BEMUTATÓJA //////////
9. 19.00 A HYBRIDART DESIGN SHOP & CAFÉ MEGNYITÓJA /////////
16. 21.00 – 24.00 STYLEWALKER NIGHT ////////////////////
17. 18.00 AJÁNDÉK TERMINÁL DESIGN AUKCIÓ ///////////////////

PROGRAMOK

design by kissmiklos / www.kissmiklos.com
fotók: Tóth Milán, PX7 Stúdió

1051 BUDAPEST; ERZSÉBET TÉR 13.
www.designterminal.hu
facebook.com/designterminal

31 TAMARA BARNOFF | 12 000 Ft

BLACK HELENA HAJPÁNT

HAJPÁNT / 25 CM / BÁRSONY

Tamara Barnoff, a grúz származású divattervezőnő hét éve él Budapesten és egyre népszerűbb a hazai divatéletben. Kreálmányai leginkább kiegészítőkből ismertek, de egyre többen szeretik ruhakollekcióit is, melyek a századeleges több évszázados átvételeket merítenek, az elegánsabb friss megújhenokkal ötvözi női ruhatárát adják. Gyöngyözi hajpántot készített az Ajándék Terminál aukciójára.

32 THE BÉTA VERSION | 39 000 Ft

PIXELFOLK3 SPECIAL EDITION TÁSKA

TÁSKA / 36X30X6 CM / NÖVÉNYI CSERZÉSŰ MARHABŐR

A The Béta Version táskáját a somogyi és sárkézi madarak szőtteseek motívumai díszítik. Ennél a kivételes darabnál a táska teste puha bőrből készült, míg alja és te fogója, növényi cserzésű marhabőrből. Nem mindennapi kiegészítő, amely után biztos megfordulnak az utcán!

33 VÁGÓ RÉKA | 19 000 Ft

VINTAGE TÁSKA

TÁSKA / 13X9 CM / FA, TEXTIL

Vágó Réka az egyik legismertebb magyar cipőtervező, de nem csupán cipőket, hanem más kiegészítőket – karkötőket, táskákat, telefontokokat - is tervez. Fából készített vintage táskája rendkívül egyedi darab, és természetesen csak az az egy készült belőle, amire az Ajándék Terminál aukcióján lehet licitálni.

Támogatóink / Partnereink

DESIGN HÉT / DIGITAL STUDIO / DUROPACK / EVENT STUFF / FUNZINE / GLAMOUR ONLINE / HELLODESIGN.HU / HG.HU / MEDENCE CSOPORT / OURFASHION BLOG / PESTIEST / POSI T1ON / PX7 STÚDIÓ / SHOPGUARD / STILBLOG / STYLEWALKER / TOPLISTA STÍLUS MAGAZIN / T-QUICK REKLÁMSZERVÍZ / VECTRA-LINE PLUS KFT. / WHERE / WILCO KFT.

Ajándék Terminál

Ajandék Terminál

Ajandék Terminál

HANDWRITTEN

This section collects highly unique typefaces that are either handwritten or doodled free style. They may be rawly developed, but they always clearly convey the personality of the brand in an assertive and visionary way. Pencil, pen, ink, and tape are used to create memorable graphics that intrigue people to embrace the brand.

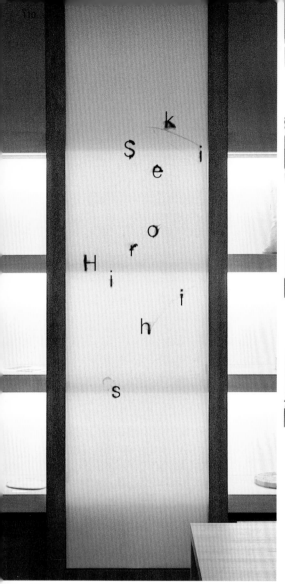

Hiroshi Seki Exhibition

The project was an exhibition of interior designer Hiroshi Seki's product design. Using a dripping treatment on the of "Seki Hiroshi", Nakano Design has expressed Seki's methodology, which combines both elements of craftsmanship and industrial design into one identity for the exhibition.

Client: Seki Design Studio
Design Agency: Nakano Design Office
Art Direction: Takeo Nakano
Design: Takeo Nakano
Fonts in Use: Linotype Univers

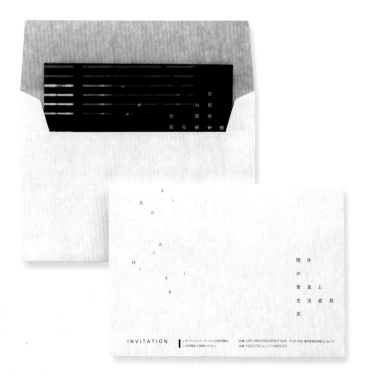

Hiroshi Seki Exhibition

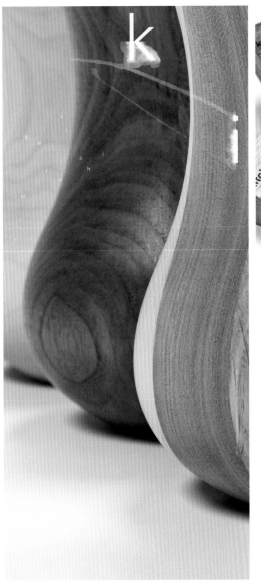

HANDWRITTEN

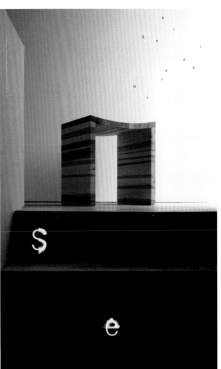

Hiroshi Seki Exhibition

HANDWRITTEN

CROQUIS

JNBY, a fashion brand in existence since 1994, recently launched CROQUIS, a new high-end menswear brand. It quickly attracted educated young men with the spiritual awakening consciousness, thanks to its distinctive design style and valuable concept. Young people who appreciate a humanistic spirit and unique way of life can find these in CROQUIS with a high degree of resonance.

Client: JNBY
Design Agency: Bobchen Design Office Hangzhou
Design: Bob Chen
Fonts in Use: Bespoke

严谨 奢华
幽默 经典
诡异 工装
诗意 生活

CROQUIS

Nobile N.00

Nobile is a contemporary members' club located at the Royal Opera House in Stockholm. Frankenstein helped develop the concept and create a visual identity for the club.

Client: Nobile
Design Agency: Frankenstein Studio
Creative Direction: Pontus Frankenstein
Photography: Pål Allan
Fonts in Use: Handwriting

Sita Murt

Sita Murt's new identity reflects its approach to fashion: simplicity, timelessness and creativity. With this in mind, an identity in black and white was chosen, with an element of versatile application: a disorderly line that indicates a restless spirit and readiness to experiment.

Client: Sita Murt
Design Agency: Clase bcn
Creative Direction: Daniel Ayuso
Design: Daniel Ayuso, Mirja Jacobs
Fonts in Use: New Baskerville

Sita Murt

Sita Murt

HANDWRITTEN

TOPSHOP

Topshop Chicago

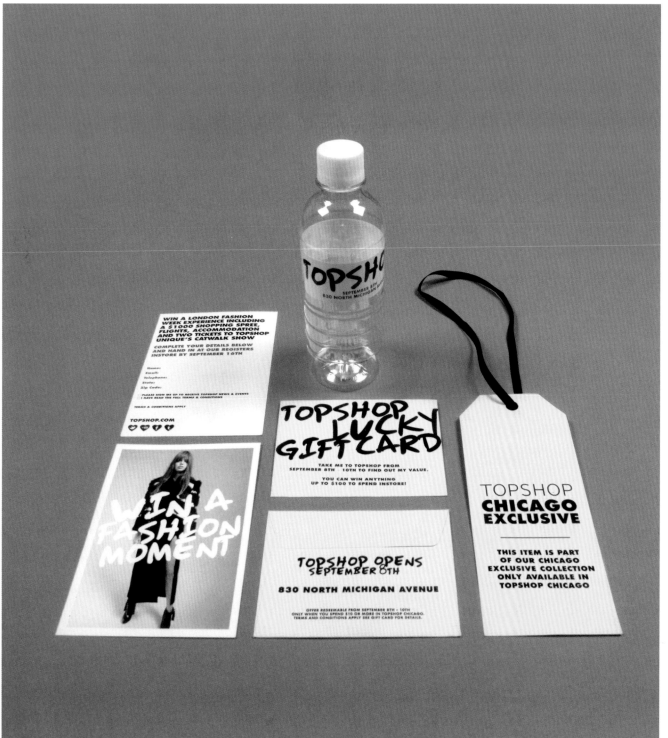

HANDWRITTEN

Topshop Chicago

Johanna Bonnevier created material for press and marketing of a new Topshop store opening in Chicago.

Client: Topshop
Design: Johanna Bonnevier
Illustration: Johanna Bonnevier
Fonts in Use: Mizike/ Gotham

POMY

TYMOTE developed the branding design for the artist shop, "POMY", which collects, showcases, and sells artwork by young designers. The agency art directed the identity, designed the shop, and undertook the planning of the project.

Client: POMY
Design Agency: TYMOTE
Fonts in Use: Custom made fonts/ Helvetica (for ad)

Êdesu Yan
no
Mise desuYan
=
Pirates
Of
Mise desu
Yan

POMY

HANDWRITTEN

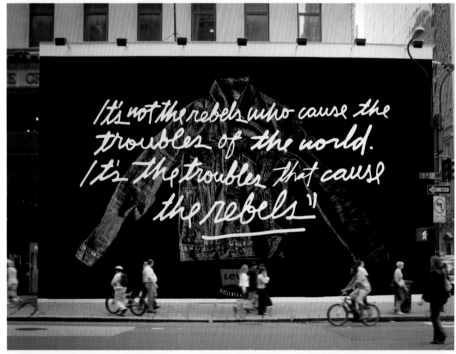

Levi's. Rebels with a Cause (Spec Work)

A true social responsibility campaign.

Pitch for Social Responsibility Global Campaign.

The main mission of the campaign was to create a platform where activists and "rebels with a cause" could join and generate local changes on a global scale.

Sunday Morning NY was involved in the art direction, product photography, design & digital Strategy.

Client: Levi's
Design Agency: Agency Heart
Creative Direction: Carlos Perez, Lewis Sempertegui
Art Direction & Design: Daniel Arenas
Planner: Jaime Dávila
Digital Strategist: Leonardo Román
Producer: Daniel Roversi
Videographer: Harry García

HANDWRITTEN

Levi's. Rebels with a Cause. (Spec Work)

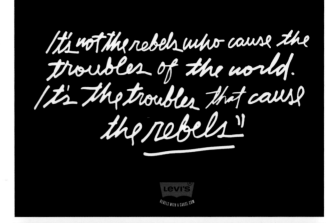

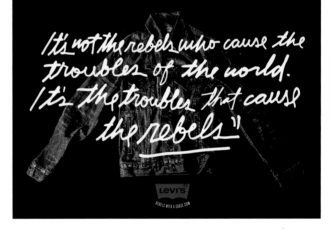

HANDWRITTEN

Levi's. Rebels with a Cause. (Spec Work)

Denim+

IYA were commissioned to create an exciting and unique brand identity and visual style for this new start-up. They wanted to create a brand that had a multi-layered approach that could illustrate the craftsmanship that goes into making a fine pair of jeans. The solution was to use indigo inks to paint simplified icons and marry them with a strong set of logotypes.

Client: Denim+
Design Agency: IYA Studio
Design: Matt Cottis

Denim+

Denim+

NIKE Basketball - The World is Watching

HORT worked on a NIKE street basketball event in New York City named "The world is watching."

HORT designed the type treatment, a font, several shoeboxes (for different districts of NYC) and a huge mural announcement for the event.

Client: NIKE
Design Agency: HORT
Art Direction (NIKE): Michael Spoljaric
Fonts in Use: NIKE NY TAPE

HANDWRITTEN

ABCDEFGHIJKLMNOP
QRSTUVWXYZ!$?.,:
1234567890 HORT

NIKE Basketball - The World is Watching

Rock the Vote

Apartment One teamed up with Rock the Vote and Simon Isaacs to develop the brand and identity for the "We Will" campaign, one of the largest non-partisan youth voter campaigns in history. To respond to Rock the Vote's goal of registering 1.5 million voters and engaging millions to turn out on election day, Apartment One created a compelling and encouraged youths to make their voices heard in the election.

The campaign combines a strong message with raw, youthful photography and hand-drawn graphical elements, to illustrate the voice of the people and create a visual dialogue between "they" and "we". The campaign visuals were kept minimal in color and graphics to heroize the They/We messaging. Apartment One was inspired by trends in youth activism and branding to build a campaign that reflected the vision behind We Will, stayed true to Rock the Vote's mission, and that could be shared virally.

Client: Rock the Vote
Design Agency: Apartment One
Creative Direction: Spencer Bagley, Liza Lowinger, Simon Isaacs
Design: Spencer Bagley, Dean Nicastro
Project Coordination: Raima McDaniel
Fonts in Use: Liberator/ Typewriter Elite

HANDWRITTEN

Rock the Vote

HANDWRITTEN

The Collection

The Collection is a restaurant, cultural space, and retail shop in one. Mind Design created the identity, signage system and all printed material. The idea for the identity relates to multiple prints, limited editions and artist signatures. The execution is relatively simple: Everything is based on an A5 format with punched holes. Mind Design used screen printing which allowed them to change colors on the printing bed, making each print unique. The larger signs are made up of A5 boards and the thickness is achieved by hanging several signs in front of each other. For the logo they asked the client to write the name in unique handwriting to connect two dots equivalent to the punched holes.

Client: The Collection
Design Agency: Mind Design
Fonts in Use: Custom-designed handwriting/ Typewriter Elite

The Collection

The Collection

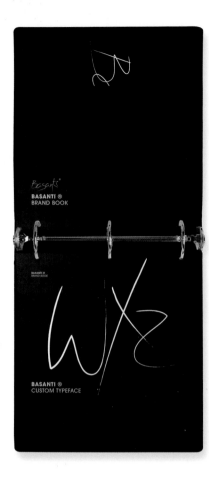

Basanti

Basanti is a gourmet tea brand in Mexico, targeted toward a premium audience. The brand belief rediscovers wellness as a modern luxury. MENOSUNOCEROUNO'S role launching the brand was creating a unique visual language combining glossy and matte surfaces on a minimal black and white palette as a canvas for a bespoke handwritten typeface that composes the logo. The relaxed traces of the logo possess a strong tension with the polished surfaces of the packages.

Client: Basanti
Design Agency: MENOSUNOCEROUNO
Creative Direction: Gerardo Ortiz
Photography: Jennifer Lucey-Brzoza
Fonts in Use: Bespoke handmade typeface

Basanti

Geist

The fantastic restaurant Geist was opened in spring, 2011 by Michelin star chef Bo Bech. The restaurant is in the beautiful "Kongens Nytorv" square in the very center of Copenhagen. Geist serves Nordic food, Nordic ingredients with a beautiful twist. ATWTP worked closely with Mr. Bech to develop the identity. Symbols representing the restaurant, the food and the poetry of the atmosphere are made as watercolor illustrations. It was so much joy in making these!

Client: Restaurant Geist
Design Agency: All the Way to Paris
Fonts in Use: Handwriting

Bondir

Evoking a dashing rabbit, the gestural word mark captures a handmade and artistic approach combining simplicity, texture and motion throughout the restaurant collateral.

Client: Bondir
Design Agency: Oat
Design: Jennifer Lucey-Brzoza
Photography: Jennifer Lucey-Brzoza
Fonts in Use: Hand Painted logo/ Didot italic

Bondir

135

Bondir

MUJI Xmas 2011

Art direction for the Christmas 2011 global campaign. In order to convey the dynamism of a marketplace, the theme of the graphics was handwritten text in chalk on a blackboard. In the video, the sounds of striking, tearing and dropping, and many other sounds that are made when you use MUJI products, were coordinated to create a percussion-style rendition of "Joy to the World". The music was produced by Shugo Tokumaru.

Client: Ryohin Keikaku Co.,Ltd.
Design Agency: Daikoku Design Institute, the Nippon Design Center, inc.
Creative Direction: Kenya Hara
Art Direction: Daigo Daikoku
Design: Daigo Daikoku, Takao Minamidate
Photography: Takaya Sakano
Copywriting: Ryo Hasumi
Music: Shugo Tokumaru
Movie: Risa Sakamoto
Fonts in Use: Helvetica MB101

MUJI Xmas 2011

MUJI Xmas 2009

Art direction for the Christmas 2009 global campaign. About a hundred people were photographed from above, forming graphics and text as they moved around. This concept is realized in posters, video, advertisements, catalog, POP, in-store display, web, etc. The resulting video conveys the beauty of organic movement.

Client: Ryohin Keikaku Co., Ltd.
Design Agency: Daikoku Design Institute, the Nippon Design Center, inc.
Creative Direction: Kenya Hara
Art Direction: Daigo Daikoku
Design: Daigo Daikoku
Photography: Akihiro Ito
Movie: Risa Sakamoto
Fonts in Use: Helvetica MB101

MUJI Xmas 2009

HANDWRITTEN

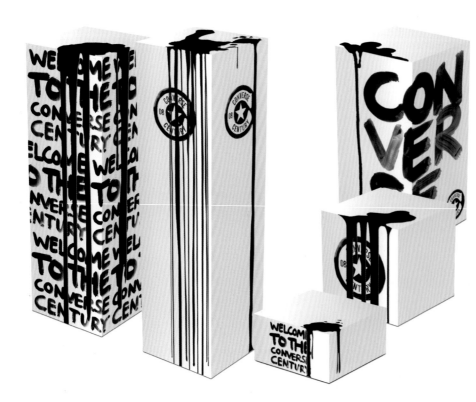

Converse

Converse

"Famous icons connected by Chucks" was the brand campaign developed by Anomaly in New York. Converse Inc. approached …,staat creative agency to develop a design direction and retail concept for Europe, as well as directing the rollout and location of the campaign. The design direction utilized the existing identity and visual language, and …,staat introduced raw, organic and fluid elements in order to balance the clean and consistent imagery. …,staat used personal handwriting, opaque paint and semitransparent ink in striking black and white. These elements were taken to the next level for the retail concept: painted quotes, black-dipped objects and high-gloss white displays brought the Converse icon to life.

Client: Converse
Design Agency: …, staat creative agency
Photography: Converse, …,staat creative agency
Fonts in Use: Handwriting

Converse

IN 1853 LEVI STRAUSS & CO. WAS BORN. LEVI STRAUSS AND JACOB DAVIS INVENTED THE FIRST BLUE JEAN AND INTRODUCED DENIM TO THE WORLD. OUR FIRST JEANS WORKED HARD, HAD A PURPOSE. TIME PASSED AND JEANS BECAME FASHION, MOVING FROM THE MINES TO THE STREETS, BUT ONE THING NEVER CHANGED:

OUR JEANS HAVE ALWAYS BEEN BUILT FOR THE PIONEERS, PAST AND PRESENT. PEOPLE WHO SPEAK THEIR MINDS, MAKE SOME NOISE, CHANGE THE CULTURE WE LIVE IN.

OUR HERITAGE IS OUR SOUL AND THE SPIRIT OF BOLDNESS LIVES THROUGH EVERY PAIR OF JEANS WE MAKE TO THIS DAY.

Levi's Packaging

Levi's Packaging

Reflecting the Levi's® store interior which is texturally rich and uses a premium palette of materials, Checkland Kindleysides created in-store packaging with a handcrafted feel.

Carrier bags and gift wrapping were developed using raw materials, an embossed logo, handwritten fonts and simple black and white photography.

Client: Levi Strauss
Design Agency: Checkland Kindleysides
Fonts in Use: Bespoke

Levi's Packaging

HANDWRITTEN

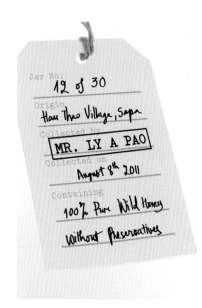

Jar No.
12 of 30
Origin
Hau Thao Village, Sapa
Collected by
MR. LY A PAO
Collected on
August 8th 2011
Containing
100% Pure Wild Honey

without Preservatives

The Hill Station

The Hill Station is a business marriage of a fine dining restaurant and deli/ boutique, located in Sapa, Vietnam's highest region. The client wanted a brand which both was reminiscent of the essence of French Indo-chine days while standing independently as a contemporary identity. The hill station products range from fresh produce harvested straight from local farms, limited packaged delicacies such as wild honey, and rice wine, to gourmet charcuteries or handmade silverware. At the same time, its signature restaurant is a renovated French outpost, with a view from the clouds.

Client: The Hill Station
Design Agency: Studio Egregius
Creative Direction: Le Huy Anh
Design: Le Huy Anh, Doan Thanh Quynh, Doan Thanh Quynh
Illustration: Bui Thi Huynh Ly
Fonts in Use: Elementa/ Elementric

HANDWRITTEN

pure homebrew rice wine for those who loves from the roof of indochine

The Hill Station

450ml

The Hill Station

The Hill Station

HTC

It's weird to have a typeface that's based on your handwriting, especially when it's on a huge billboard in Times Square. Back in 2009, Figtree rebranded HTC and came up with the strap line, "quietly brilliant". The whole identity approach was based on a hand drawn, doodled style, which gave HTC a really friendly, human feel. Figtree wanted the brand to have a less techy feel than the other telecoms companies out there. After drawing "quietly brilliant", Figtree drew the entire typeface. It involved hours of sitting down at a desk writing endless a's, b's, c's, though to z's. Uppercase and lowercase. Not to mention all the global variations. It was a year spent holding a trusted black "Sign" pen by Pilot.

Client: HTC
Design Agency: Figtree
Creative Direction: Nick Couch
Design: Nahim Afzal, Lucie Raufast
Photography: Hector Porric
Typographer: Miles Newlyn
Fonts in Use: HTC Hand

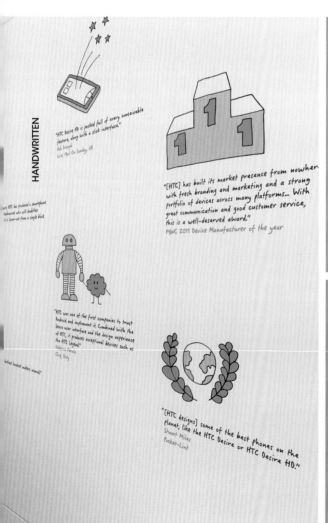

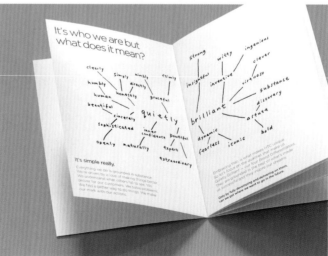

HTC

EXPERIMENTAL

Typefaces serve an important role in carrying out the meanings and mood of language. Experimental typefaces created from geometric shapes, letter segments, and pixels intrigue people to explore connotations and appreciate text as image.

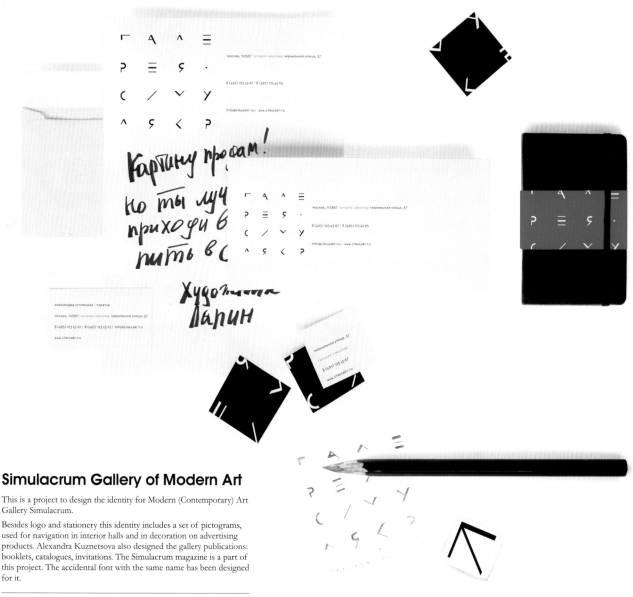

Simulacrum Gallery of Modern Art

This is a project to design the identity for Modern (Contemporary) Art Gallery Simulacrum.

Besides logo and stationery this identity includes a set of pictograms, used for navigation in interior halls and in decoration on advertising products. Alexandra Kuznetsova also designed the gallery publications: booklets, catalogues, invitations. The Simulacrum magazine is a part of this project. The accidental font with the same name has been designed for it.

Client: Simulacrum Gallery of Modern Art
Design: Alexandra Kuznetsova
Font Simulacrum: Alexandra Kuznetsova
Fonts in Use: Identity: FF OCR-F (FontShop International)

Simulacrum Gallery of Modern Art

Børk

For this final project at the Iceland Academy of the Arts, Thorleifur Gunnar Gislason created and branded a studio that makes gift wrap. He wanted the company and the gift wrapping series to be Scandinavian in look and theme. The name he chose for the creative studio is Børk, short for Börkur or Bark which means tree bark. Usage of the logo around corners in signage and on the stationery is a reference to the initial meaning of the name, i.e. to cover or conceal something. He decided to use the line crossing the Ø as a graphical element and use it as a folding line for the identity. For the stationery, business cards, envelopes and CD envelope, the logo and the folding lines create a visual interpretation of concealing something in a simple way.

Client: Self-Initiated (school project)
Design: Thorleifur Gunnar Gíslason
Fonts in Use: Agenda/ Palatino

Børk

Le Cintré & Co

Visual identity project for Le Cintré & Co, a boutique hotel that offers an atmosphere revolving around arts and urban culture, aimed at an open-minded intellectual, non-conformist and creative target clientele. The hotel space has the particularity of hosting conferences, exhibits, workshops and cultural activities. Le Cintré & Co collaborates with artists from around the globe, working in various creative spheres, to promote and contribute to its constant development. Le Cintré & Co is made up of multiple departments, sub brands and signature events, which all have specific names, functions and a logotype that support the main brand.

Client: Le Cintré & Co
Instructor: Louis Gagnon
Design: Emanuel Cohen
Fonts in Use: Futura/ Architype Renner

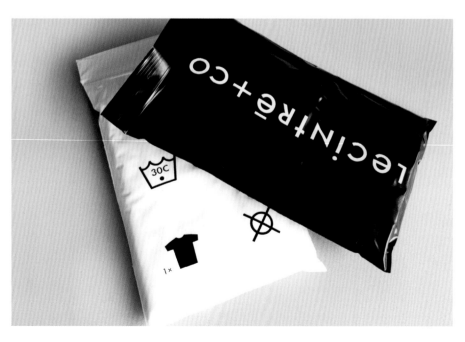

leah schmidt backward – www.leschmidt.com
séléction de la collection d'objets perdus et retrouvés
de Leah Schmidt, chercheuse allemande, 1958.

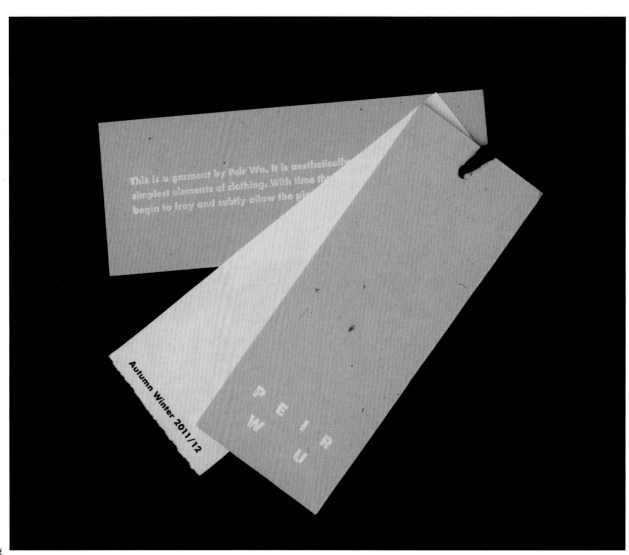

Peir Wu

Present Perfect was approached to design the visual identity of newly established menswear label Peir Wu. Peir's clothing combines sculpted shapes and modern textiles, futuristic ideals with classic concepts of knitwear. One of the main challenges was to avoid prescriptive and standard templates for fashion label identities. The final concept allows for a utilitarian, minimal and bold structure while keeping a sense of craftsmanship.

Client: Peir Wu
Design Agency: Present Perfect
Design: Ivan Markovic, Povilas Utovka
Fonts in Use: Bespoke

Peir Wu

dod magazine

Naming and visual identity for a pop music blog.
The name is just the word pop in reverse, upside
down.

Client: dod magazine
Design Agency: Andrés Requena Graphic Design
Design: Andrés Requena
Photography: Andrés Requena
Fonts in Use: Avenir

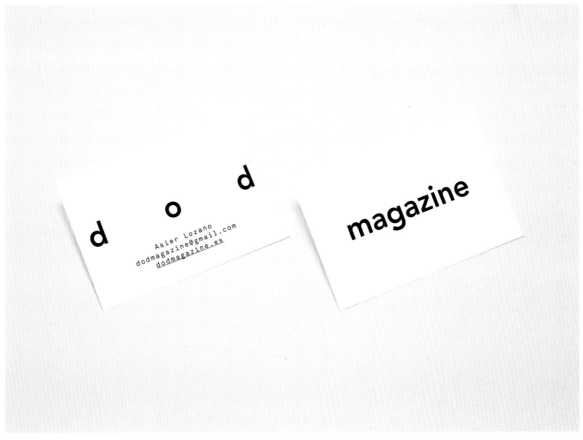

dod magazine

Departamento

Departamento is a magazine centered on design, society and art. Several concept issues were created for their first editorial run. Derek Kim was approached to conceptualize an identity that would emphasize the creative nature of this magazine with intricate layouts and a flexible grid system. Therefore, the Departamento identity follows a playful aesthetic, where the main logotype is always able to be broken in different ways. This allows designers to freely manipulate the identity into their own hands. Additional elements for promotional purposes were designed using a similar "broken-grid" system.

Client: Departamento
Design Agency: Network Osaka
Creative Direction: You vs. Me
Design: Derek Kim
Editorial Design: You vs. Me
Production: Gordon Hewitt
Fonts in Use: OCR-B

DEPARTAMENTO magazine
design / society / art

third issue
january 2009

contents:
— public defacement
— comfortable?
— design wants
— discussion forum
— moving neue grafik

USA — $20.00
CAN — $16.00

copy _____ of 1,000

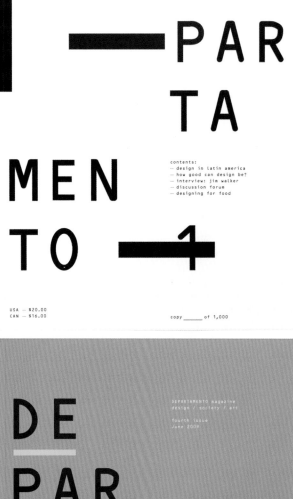

DEPARTAMENTO magazine
design / society / art

first issue
january 2008

contents:
— design in latin america
— how good can design be?
— interview: jim walker
— discussion forum
— designing for food

USA — $20.00
CAN — $16.00

copy _____ of 1,000

DEPARTAMENTO magazine
design / society / art

second issue
june 2008

contents:
— visual poetry
— not design
— hatevertising
— discussion forum
— the mailbox

USA — $20.00
CAN — $16.00

copy _____ of 1,000

DEPARTAMENTO magazine
design / society / art

fourth issue
june 2009

contents:
— under 21
— propaganda
— aeropuerto: airline livery design
— discussion forum
— designing for food

USA — $20.00
CAN — $16.00

copy _____ of 1,000

EXPERIMENTAL

Departamento

DESK——IDEA
DESK——IDEA
DESK——IDEA
DESK—IDEA

DESK——IDEA

Deskidea

Deskidea is a Barcelona-based office supplies e-commerce venue with a main aim: to provide customers with a sense of simplicity during their first purchase from the Deskidea website.

The brand was designed to boost this simplicity value and the graphic solution came from the name itself, Deskidea. The idea was to convey its value using basic office utensils, with a pencil as the main icon.

The different corporate applications are based on the pencil as a symbol, operating by itself or embedded within the brand.

Client: Deskidea
Design Agency: LARSSON•DUPREZ
Design: Alex Dalmau
Photography: Susana Gellida
Fonts in Use: Avenir lt std

Deskidea

EXPERIMENTAL

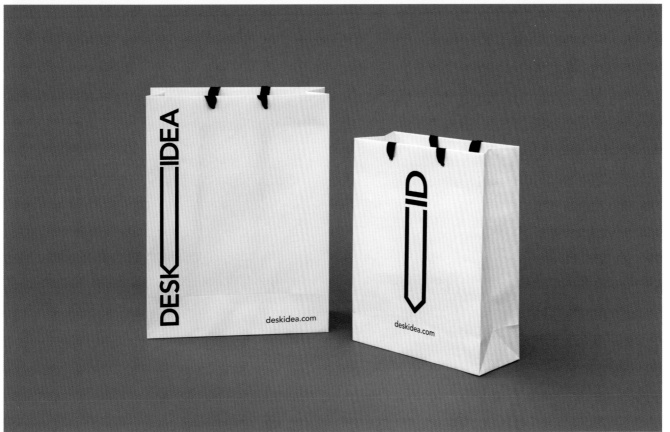

Deskidea

Neue Galerie

The Neue Galerie in New York has a collection of German/Austrian art and design. Inspired by an iconic piece from the collection, "The Kiss," by Gustav Klimt, which features highly abstracted color planes and figures, Yooin Cho developed a modular identity and word mark for the museum based on items in the collection. It has been used to brand exhibitions, programs, and events.

Client: Neue Galerie
Creative Direction: Joe Marianek
Art direction & Design: Yooin Cho
Fonts in Use: MrEaves/ Gotham

EXPERIMENTAL

Neue Galerie

Neue Galerie

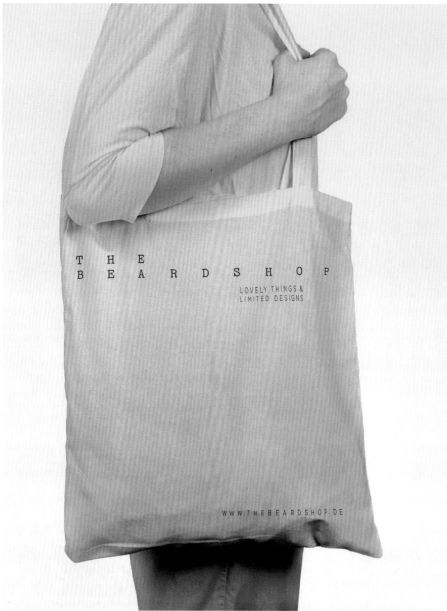

The Beardshop – Online Store

For the online shop THE BEARDSHOP, which sells design, art and fashion products in small and strictly limited editions, I LIKE BIRDS developed the corporate image, which aims to present these products individually applying a wide range of colors based on Johannes Itten´s color theory. To achieve this, designers used different coloured paper for printing purposes. The website builds on this concept and the respective products are emphasised by the various colours used.

Client: The Beardshop
Design Agency: I LIKE BIRDS
Coding of the website: Thomas Lempa
Fonts in Use: The Beardshop Superslim

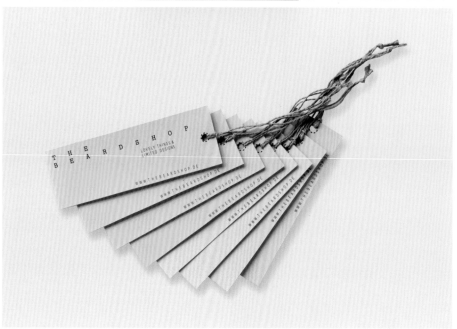

The Beardshop - Online Store

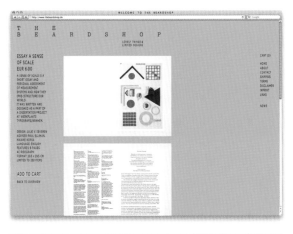

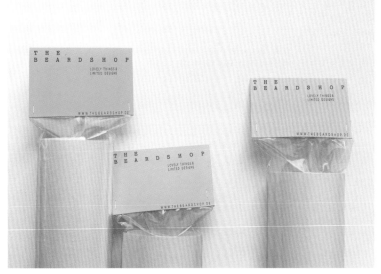

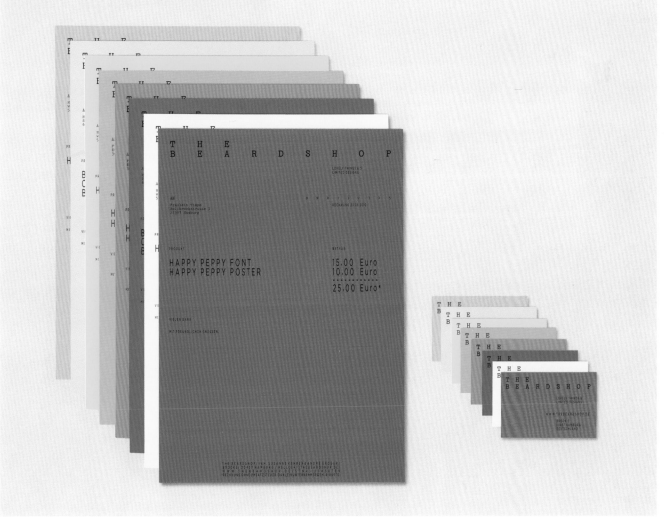

The Beardshop – Online Store

Filler Shirts & Tapes

Logotype for post-hardcore band Filler
from Belgium. The logo is used on
several applications, such as shirts, a flag,
a tape.

Client: Filler
Design: Ward Heirwegh
Fonts in Use: Apercu Bold

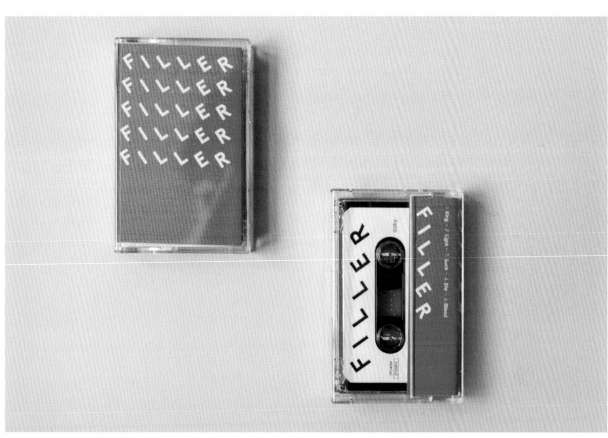

Filler Shirts & Tapes

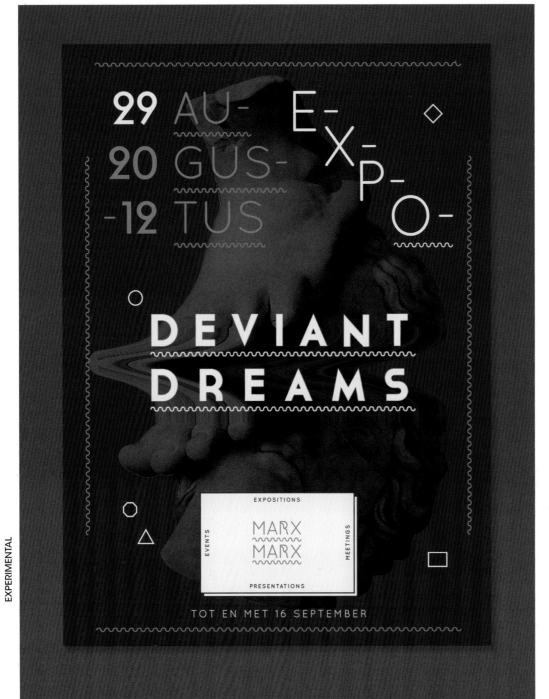

Marx Marx

Marx Marx is a fictional project, inspired by a similar studio space where Mark Niemeijer did an internship. He wanted to create an original appearance equal to the function of the studio.

Client: Self-initiated
Design Agency: YOUMAAN
Design: Mark Niemeijer
Fonts in Use: Bespoke
(Quicksand twisted)

EXPERIMENTAL

Marx Marx

Marx Marx

3.3 FIELD TRIP®

Identity for 3.3 Field Trip

Identity design for the new fashion brand 3.3 Field Trip, including the brand name, logotype, and design of various applications. From maps to weather forecasts, a set of graphic elements was designed and utilized as building blocks of the logotype and pattern design.

Client: ALAND
Design Agency: studio fnt
Creative Direction: Jaemin Lee, Heesun Kim
Design: Sue Park
Fonts in Use: Bespoke

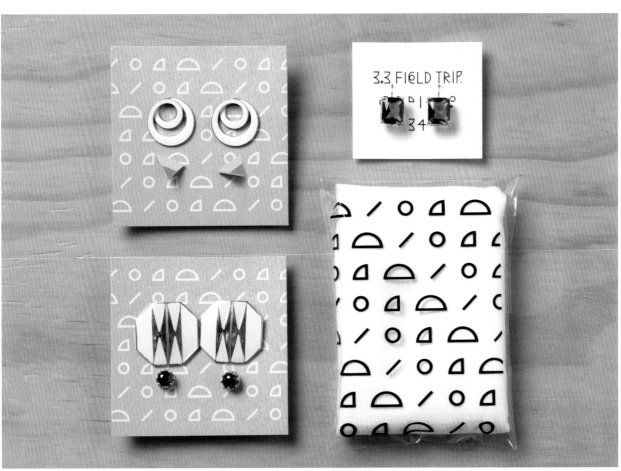

Identity for 3.3 Field Trip

Carpet Sign

Carpet Sign is one of the leading producers of high-end design rugs. Studio Laucke Siebein was asked to develop a new brand strategy, visual identity and a re-design for all its communication tools and product presentations as well. Within an accurately defined creative concept based on a fresh and sober no-nonsense approach, all items become a dignified representative of the beautiful and precious products of Carpet Sign.

Client: Carpet Sign
Design Agency: Studio Laucke Siebein
Creative Direction: Dirk Laucke and Johanna Siebein in cooperation with Christiane Müller
Design: Dirk Laucke and Johanna Siebein
Design and art direction for Carpet Sign interior and stand projects: Bas van Tol
Fonts in Use: Futura

EXPERIMENTAL

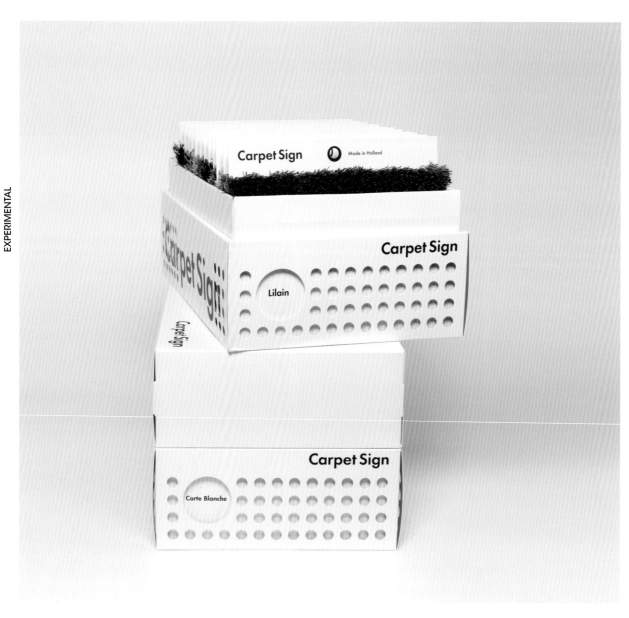

Carpet Sign

METROPOLIS

Pile height: 16 mm
Pile weight: 3700 g/m²
Material: 80% polyester — 20% New Zealand wool
Design: Carpet Sign Studio

COLOURS
Christiane Müller

Colour highlights run parallel to the short side of the rug.
The design will be adopted to the size
of the custom made rug.
Minimum length of a Metropolis design rug is two metres.

Colours also available in uni.

Metropolis 220060

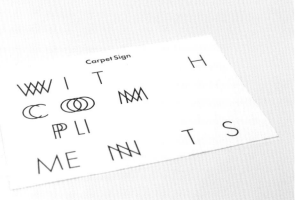

Metropolis 220120

The Lollipop Shoppe

StudioMakgill was asked to help The Lollipop Shoppe take its next step to create an identity built on innovation, personality and refined aesthetics. The designers wanted to create something to reflect the heritage of their large line of classic products from manufacturers like Vitra, which fit in with the contemporary brands like Established & Sons and convey the straightforward nature with which The Lollipop Shoppe conducts its business. StudioMakgill created a bespoke stencil typeface (partly inspired by the 20th century modular stencils created by Josef Albers and Le Corbusier, but with a contemporary elegance) that is used throughout the identity.

Client: The Lollipop Shoppe
Design Agency: StudioMakgill
Interior Design: Found Associates
Fonts in Use: Lollipop (bespoke)/ Akkurat/ Elementa

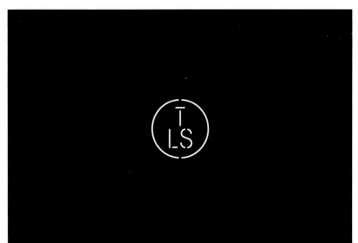

EXPERIMENTAL

DOWNSTAIRS
↙

Furniture, Lighting
& Storage

The Lollipop Shoppe

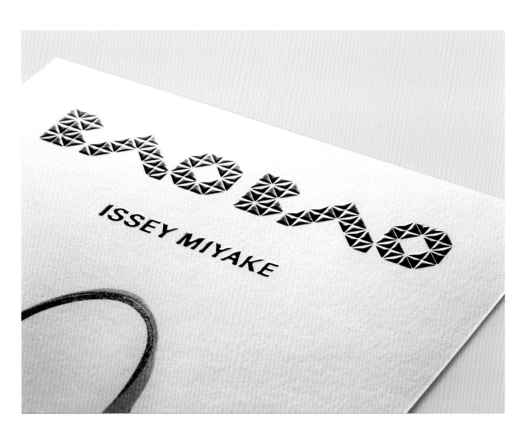

BAO BAO
ISSEY MIYAKE

These are DM card and tag designs for BAO BAO ISSEY MIYAKE. Taku Satoh Design took the structure of the bag based on a basic triangular pattern and applied it into the production process of the BAO BAO logo. Additionally, they incorporated the numerous unique logos that were created in the process of the logo production into the visual. The significance of these design are that an infinite number of different bags can be created from this single basic pattern. The method of defining a rule to create an infinite number of ideas is the same as the Haiku rule of 5-7-5 that has enabled the composition of an eternal number of poems.

Client: ISSEY MIYAKE INC.
Design Agency: Taku Satoh Design Office Inc.
Art Direction: Taku Satoh
Design: Shingo Noma
Photography: Yasuaki Yoshinaga
Fonts in Use: Original

EXPERIMENTAL

BAO BAO ISSEY MIYAKE

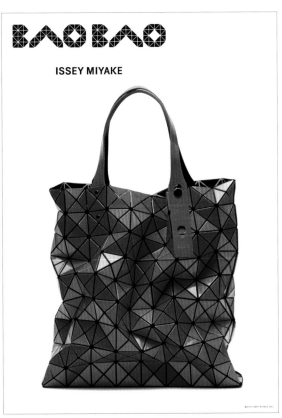

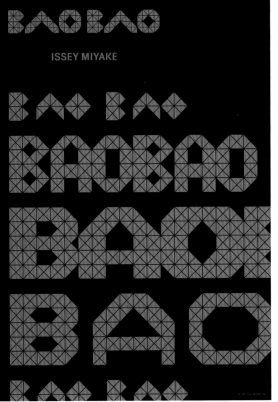

EXPERIMENTAL

Bulbo.

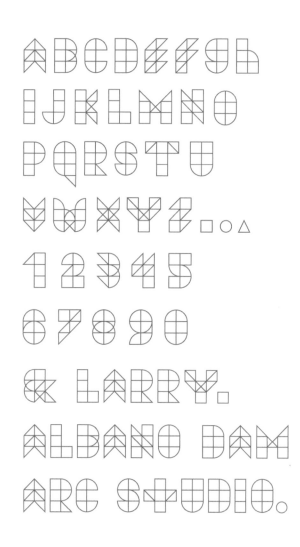

EXPERIMENTAL

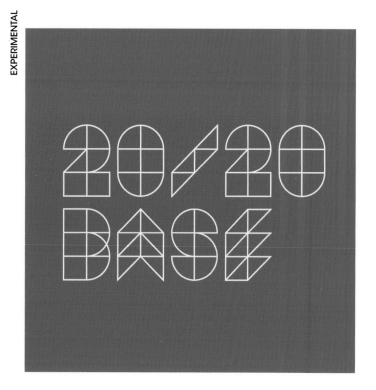

20/20

Base was the fourth installment of the landmark exhibition 20/20 started in 2004 by the DesignSingapore Council featuring 20 Singaporean creators and designers. This exhibition explored the base of the designer's self, process, concepts, media and artworks. The basic shapes of a square, circle and triangle were therefore the inspiration for the typography.

Client: DesignSingapore Council
Design Agency: Black Design
Creative Direction: Jackson Tan
Fonts in Use: Bespoke

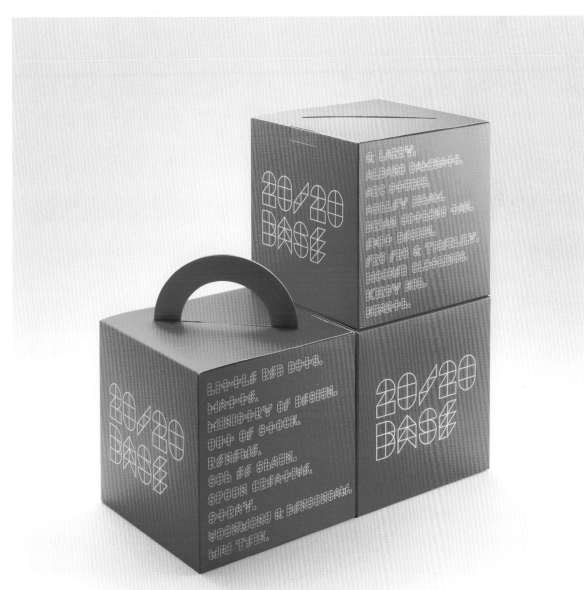

Gramercy Flower Shop

This is a re-designed form for Gramercy flower shop. To inform the public of the shop's services, different hues are used for different occasions to catch the eye of passersby.

Client: School of Visual Arts
Design Direction: Paula Scher
Design: Jiwon Kim

Gramercy Flower Shop

Gramercy Flower Shop

Belmacz

Belmacz is a London based jewelry company that opened its first shop and gallery in London Mayfair. For the launch, Mind Design re-designed the original identity and worked in collaboration with Jump Studios on the interior. The new identity takes the original logo (which has been in use for about 8 years) but adds a variety of thicker, "raw" letter shapes. Those shapes relate to the process in which raw minerals and diamonds are more and more refined until they become a piece of jewelry. The visual references start with the mines, go to the raw materials, the raw letter shapes and in the end to the refined letter shapes of the original logo.

Client: Belmacz
Design Agency: Mind Design
Interior Design: Jump Studios
Fonts in Use: Custom-made font/ Minion

Belmacz

Belmacz

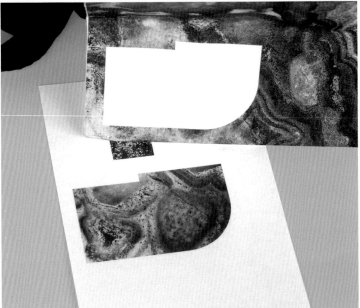

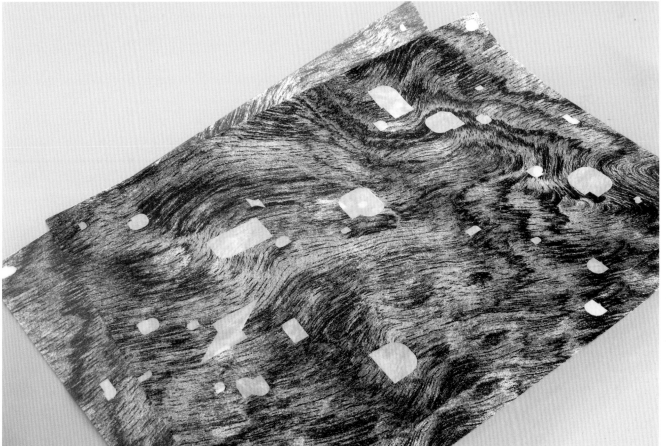

EXPERIMENTAL

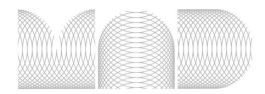

Identity for Museum of Arts and Design (MAD)

Michael Bierut of Pentagram created a new identity for the Museum of Arts and Design (MAD). The MAD acronym is a great asset: it is short, pronounceable and memorable. Michael and his team wanted a way of writing the name that could embody the value of the museum, something that seemed inventive and that could be utilized for in different occasions. The simple forms of the new logo permit just that kind of transformation. Pentagram developed an entire alphabet and numbers, based on the basic MAD combination made out of squares and circles, called MAD Face. The typeface reflects the spirit of MAD and is used in special promotions. A more conventional typeface, Futura, is used in print applications and signage.

Client: Museum of Arts and Design
Design Agency: Pentagram
Art Direction: Michael Bierut/ Pentagram
Design: Michael Bierut, Joe Marianek
Fonts in Use: Custom font/ Futura

museum of arts and design

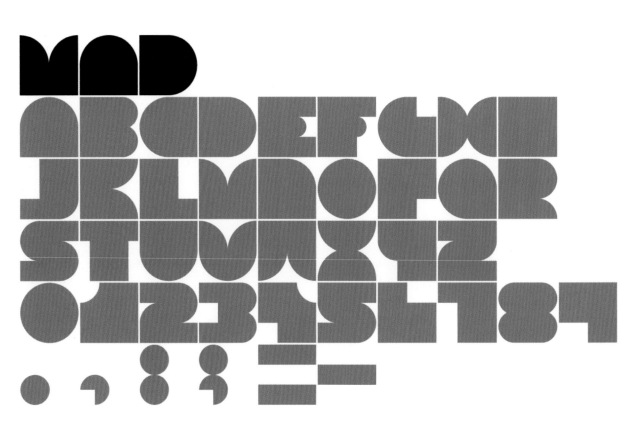

Identity for Museum of Arts and Design (MAD)

Raul Santos

MOOD®
Lamp Design & Lighting Concept

Rua Adriano Canas nº 19 2740-003
Porto Salvo, Portugal
(+351) 214218600
info@mood.pt

www.mood.pt

Filipa Maia
Designer
filipamaia@mood.pt

MOOD®
Lamp Design & Lighting Concept

Rua Adriano Canas nº 19 2740-003
Porto Salvo, Portugal
(+351) 214218600
info@mood.pt

www.mood.pt

Rita Muralha
Arquitecta
(+351) 919 601 737
ritamuralha@mood.pt

MOOD®
Lamp Design & Lighting Concept

Rua Adriano Canas nº 19 2740-003
Porto Salvo, Portugal
(+351) 214218600
info@mood.pt

www.mood.pt

EXPERIMENTAL

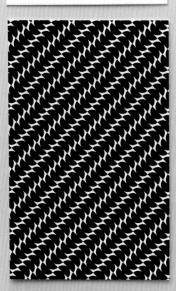

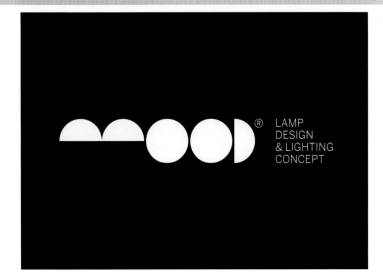

MOOD

Visual identity system for MOOD/ Lamp design
& Lighting concept. Printed at M2. The identity
was based on the MOOD® lamps modular design
process. Exploring the movement created by
repetition of a basic shape was the objective for
the identity, represented in patterns, typography,
illustration, etc.

Client: MOOD
Design Agency: MAGA - atelier
Design: José Mendes/ MAGA
Fonts in Use: Original typeface designed by José
Mendes and Benton Sans

MOOD

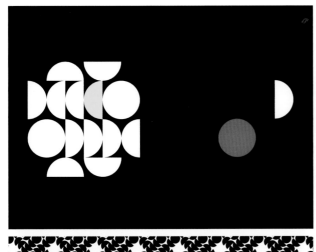

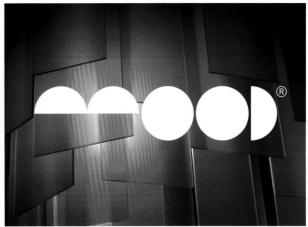

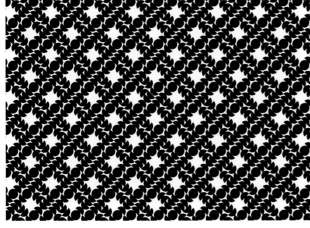

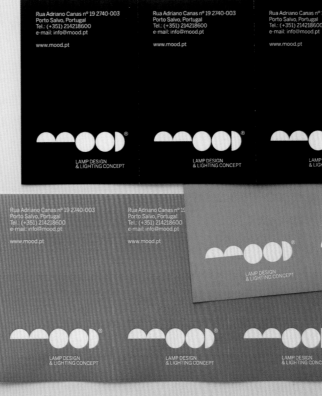

MOOD

MINIMAL

San serif typefaces are naturally neutral, clear, and accessible. This type choice is one distinctive path to reduce graphic elements and instead focus on typography in order to create a strong visual impact for the project and brand. The spacing between the letters holds the most important information, allowing people to focus, taste, and indulge in the end result.

Design Museum x State of the Obvious® Collection

Extending the philosophy & thinking behind our branded State of the Obvious® Collection, Mash Creative designed a set of products exclusively for the Design Museum.

The design of these products has been heavily influenced by the International Typographic Style from the 1950s and '60s and shows an evolution from our original S/O/T/O collection. It has been designed to appeal to typography and design lovers alike.

S/O/T/O designs and produces products which not only look good but also have a useful function. The exclusive Design Museum collection consists of iPhone 3 & 4 and iPad 1 & 2 GelaSkins, Staedtler Marker Pens, USB Sticks, Travel Card Wallets and Key Rings.

Client: Design Museum x State of the Obvious® Collection
Design Agency: Mash Creative
Fonts in Use: AG Schoolbook/ Georgia

Design Museum x State of the Obvious® Collection

State of the Obvious Collection

With consumerism at an all time high and brand image playing an ever more important role in consumers' buying choices, Mash Creative felt an overwhelming desire to challenge what has become "The Norm."

At Mash Creative they believe there is a niche in the market for a collection of products which turns conventional branding on its head. S/O/T/O (State of the Obvious) is a range of merchandise and apparel which does just that. S/O/T/O uses the product's description to create a unique brand identity.

The S/O/T/O collection is designed to have a playful, modern and bold brand image which is flexible enough to be adapted across a wide variety of items. The collection will continue to grow with many other products already in the pipeline.

Client: Mash Creative
Design Agency: Mash Creative
Fonts in Use: AG Schoolbook/ Georgia

MINIMAL

State of the Obvious® Collection

MINIMAL

State of the Obvious® Collection

Pottporus

Pottporus has the aim of promoting young creatives and giving them a perspective on the industry. The business works in the fields of hip-hop and urban culture and is the umbrella for the Young Pottporus, the dance productions of Renegade, the annual autumn Pottporus festival and the Pottporus Dance School.

Client: Pottporus e.V.
Design Agency: Büro für Grafik Design
Design: Raffael Stüken
Photography: Oliver Look
Fonts in Use: Akzidenz Grotesk Bold

MINIMAL

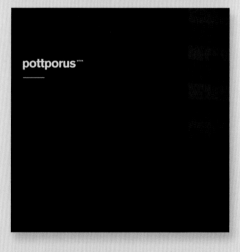

Pottporus

Good Food

Identity, packaging and branding for a healthy food brand based in Monterrey, Mexico.

Good Food has the vision of bringing taste back to fast food. Using high quality ingredients and recipes, the brand offers traditional Mexican recipes in a very easy to use frozen food format.

Face had to design a reflection of this statement with a very clean, simple, international look, to make people believe in frozen food again, now in a good way.

Client: GoodFood
Design Agency: Face
Design: Face
Fonts in Use: GoodFood Sans/ Gotham/ Bauer Bodoni

MINIMAL

Good Food

Fab Print Suite

Fab commissioned Studio Lin to make a set of printed materials to be used in each of their product mailings. We came up with a shortened "Fab" language and applied it in bold typographic way. The use of foil stamping on thick card stock and PVC helped elevate the print pieces into keepsakes.

Client: Fab
Design Agency: Studio Lin
Design: Studio Lin
Fonts in Use: Avant Garde

Pocklington Press

IYA studio were commissioned
by Pocklington Press to create the
packaging for their first major project.
Collaborating with four London based
artists, a print maker, a photographer
and IYA Studio as a design studio, the
project was to create a unique, cutting-
edge portfolio of fine art prints which
explores and expresses traditional
printmaking techniques as a reaction
to the throw away printmaking trend
of today. The brief to the four new
artists was to create fine art prints
reflecting the issues of "Unarchive the
Archive". The result was a beautiful
oversized folder which housed 25/1
archive prints which were sold as
a complete package. The outcome
is to change society's thoughts on
traditional crafts and the future of art
in print.

Client: Pocklington Press
Design Agency: IYA Studio
Design: Matt Cottis
Photography: Dylan Collard,
David Sykes
Fonts in Use: Museo/ Akzidenz

MINIMAL

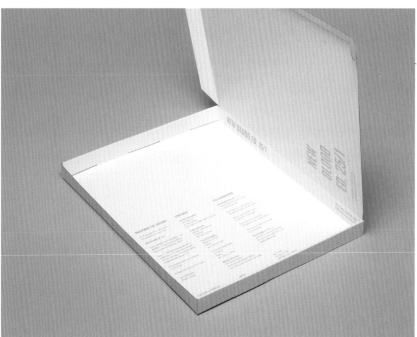

Pocklington Press

Schmidt Bros.

Schmidt Brothers is a cutlery company
based in New York. Triboro was
responsible for the branding concept
and packaging.

Client: Schmidt Brothers Cutlery
Design Agency: Triboro
Fonts in Use: Futura/ Ironclad

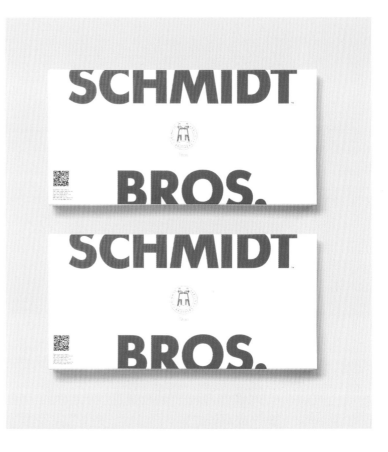

Schmidt Bros.

FEB Design Stationery

FEB Design Stationery

For their own stationery, FEB Design aimed to show the communicative quality of each one of its materials, so the media becomes the message and the central character of this assignment. The tone of the selected sentences reflects the close relationship that they nourish daily towards their customers.

Client: FEB Design
Design Agency: FEB Design, FIBA Design
Design: Marta Fragata, Miguel Batista
Fonts in Use: Flama/ Feliciano Type Foundry

MINIMAL

FEB Design Stationery

Hudson Gavin
Martin Identity

Hudson Gavin Martin is a boutique
legal practice formed by three partners,
who advise on Intellectual Property
and Technology Law. Alt Group began
a conversation that reveals "ideas" that
come in threes. The three wise men,
Hudson, Gavin, Martin, are cool, calm
and collected and advise on clients'
assets, equities, and liabilities. The
identity uses the copyright, trademark
and registered symbols to reference
their core business. The registered
symbol couldn't be used until the
logotype was registered. An interim
"launch" logotype was produced with
an asterisk and small copy (Registration
Pending) in place of the ® symbol
until registration was complete.

Client: Hudson Gavin Martin
Design Agency: Alt Group
Creative Direction: Dean Poole
Design: Clem Devine, Aaron Edwards,
Dean Poole, Tony Proffit
Photography: Duncan Cole
Fonts in Use: Helvetica Neue/ Didot

MINIMAL

Hudson Gavin Martin Identity

Hudson Gavin Martin Identity

Box Café

Box Café is located at the entry of New Zealand's largest performing arts centre. It also functions as an information centre, ticketing office and venue. The name and visual collateral needed to simply communicate the identity. The logomark is built from a series of dots that reference the design vernacular of theatre lighting and dot matrix printers, commonly found in ticket offices.

The mark lends itself to a range of executions and finishes: printed, die-cut, embossed, recessed or floated. This was extended into a broader visual language communicating the identity pictorially.

Client: The Edge
Design Agency: Alt Group
Creative Direction: Dean Poole
Designer: Toby Curnow, Janson Chau
Photography: Carlos Rodríguez
Copywriter: Dean Poole, Ben Corban
Fonts in Use: Bespoke Box Café Typeface/ Hermes (by Optimo Foundry)

Box Café

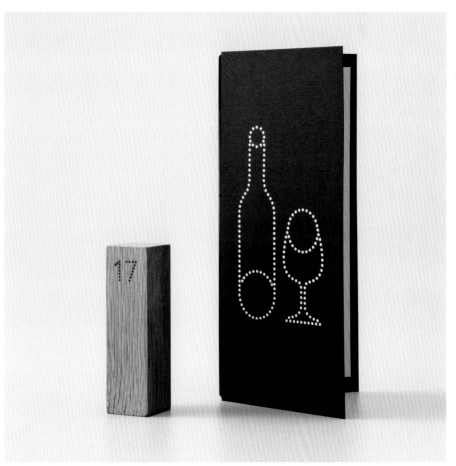

Box Café

La Vittoria Chicago

lg2boutique created the graphic platform for the prestigious La Vittoria gala, a night of gastronomic pleasure with proceeds benefitting the Quebec Breast Cancer Foundation. Chicago, the hometown of guest chef Charlie Trotter, and the glamorous art-deco style unique to the U.S. were heavy influences on the creative design of all communications, including an invitation in the shape of a cloth placemat, the room decor, the waiter/ waitress aprons, the menus and the souvenir book from the evening.

Client: Nathalie LeProhon (Honorary co-president of La Vittoria), Johanne Demers (founder of La Vittoria)
Design Agency: lg2boutique
Creative Direction: Claude Auchu
Design: Anne-Marie Clermont, Maude Lescarbeau
Copywriting: Pierre Lussier
Print production: lg2fabrique
Client Services: Marie-Claude Lacasse
Fonts in Use: Bureau Eagle Bold/ Bureau Eagle Book/ Chronicle Texte G1/ Hoefler vinum/ Hollywood deco SG Medium/ Knockout/ Manhattant ITC

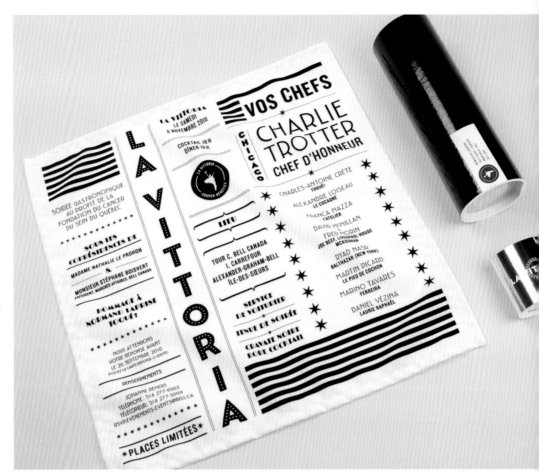

La Vittoria Chicago

La Vittoria Chicago

Bünker Bar

Bünker is one of London's few genuine micro-breweries and Ideas Factory's brief was to create a brand with a lively and inviting personality.

Utilising the overall concept of "Munich bier festival in the heart of London," they delivered strong graphics and confident, punchy copy which complemented the industrial style interior with its glowing copper brewing equipment.

Client: Bünker Bar
Design Agency: Ideas Factory
Design: MJ Jackson
Fonts in Use: Helvetica Bold 75/
Helvetica Black 95

MINIMAL

Bünker Bar

Bünker Bar

Boxpark

Boxpark's vision for creating a "community of brands" - a temporary collection of shops, cafes and galleries - functioning out of shipping containers was an exciting new concept. Set in Shoreditch, east London, an area known for a distinctly leftfield approach to retail, Boxpark aimed to raise the bar in one of the world's most creative markets.

StudioMakgill created a strong visual identity with an industrial aesthetic, reflecting the monolithic quality of the containers themselves. They designed not only the identity, website and brochures, but also managed the design and production of the directional signage, London-wide advertising campaigns and large format graphics. They continue to provide ongoing design support.

Client: Boxpark
Design Agency: StudioMakgill
Architects: We Like Today
Photography: Archard Architectural
Fonts in Use: ITC Conduit/ Deck

MINIMAL

Boxpark

Stories

In order to create a strong and totally unique café experience from concept to name, typographic profile and packaging, the identity needed to be warm, welcoming, honest and genuine and targeted to young professionals.

Black, white and stainless steel is blended with warm wood, and the old fashioned café-feel is expressed by things like a board with old, detachable letters and traditional cups and trays. The graphics are clean and simple, but at the same time surprising and playful. The design exudes personality, quality, style and a big city feeling.

Client: Turesgruppen AB
Design: BVD
Fonts in Use: Avisto

Mads Nørgaard Copenhagen – Speak Up!

Mads Nørgaard is an excellent example of how you can work strategically with a brand while breaking new ground for the fashion company and its communications. In a close collaboration with Mads Nørgaard, e-Types has developed a new brand strategy, a new visual identity, fashion shows, image campaigns, records, packaging, and fashion films.

By using elements from the world of culture referenced by Mads Nørgaard in his work and inspiration, e-Types created a more meaningful brand. The brand transgresses that transgresses ideas of high and low culture by plucking from both worlds- just like Mads Nørgaard does in his collections. The fashion company positions itself differently from its main competitors through a genuine link to its customers' cultural context, updating its relevancy to attract a new target group while linking between the past and the present.

Client: Mads Nørgaard Copenhagen
Design Agency: e-Types
Design: Jess Andersen
Photography: Frederik Lindstrom & Hasse Nielsen
Fonts in Use: Marilfrom (from PLAYTYPE)

Mads Nørgaard Copenhagen – Speak Up!

MINIMAL

http://www.plusminuszero.jp

±0

Taku Satoh Design took charge of the art direction and graphic design of the brand, which develops household electric appliances based on a new perspective; this brand started with a product designer, Mr. Naoto Fukasawa, as the producer. ±0 means design that fits the world with no misalignment.

Client: PLUS MINUS ZERO CO., LTD
Design Agency: Taku Satoh Design
Art Direction: Taku Satoh
Creative Direction: Naoto Fukasawa
Design: Taku Satoh, Ichiji Ohishi, Teppei Yuyama
Fonts in Use: Bespoke

MINIMAL

MINIMAL

ELTTOB TEP ISSEY MIYAKE/ GINZA

ELTTOB TEP ISSEY MIYAKE is a special complex store where gives customers an opportunity to enjoy shopping among ISSEY MIYAKE INC's numerous brands. ELTTOB TEP ISSEY MIYAKE/ SEMBA opened in the spring of 2007 in Osaka. This was followed by the opening of its second store ELTTOB TEP ISSEY MIYAKE/ GINZA in Ginza, Tokyo in spring of 2011. Taku Satoh Design oversees everything related to the design ranging from the naming to logo, graphics, store, furniture, window display and ads. The naming concept for ELTTOB TEP can be understood if you read it backwards. In Japan, the container used to bottle mineral water is known as PET BOTTLE. In other words, we simply reversed the name of the most common everyday object. It represents the store's concept of taking the concept of a common object and reversing it.

Client: ISSEY MIYAKE INC.
Design Agency: Taku Satoh Design Office Inc.
Art Direction: Taku Satoh
Design: Shingo Noma
Photography: Yasuaki Yoshinaga
Fonts in Use: Original

ELTTOB TEP ISSEY MIYAKE/ GINZA

MINIMAL

ELTTOB TEP ISSEY MIYAKE/ GINZA

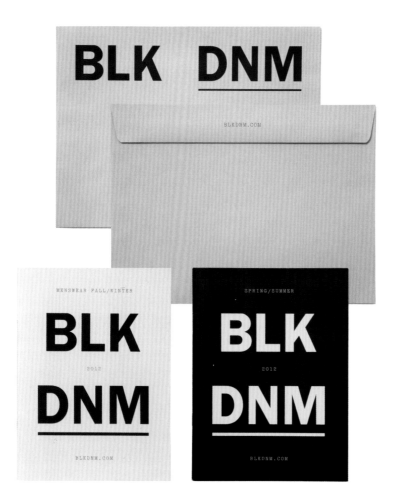

BLK DNM

BLK DNM is a new clothing company
created by Johan Lindeberg.

Client: BLK DNM
Design Agency: Triboro
Fonts in Use: Franklin Gothic/
Typewriter Elite

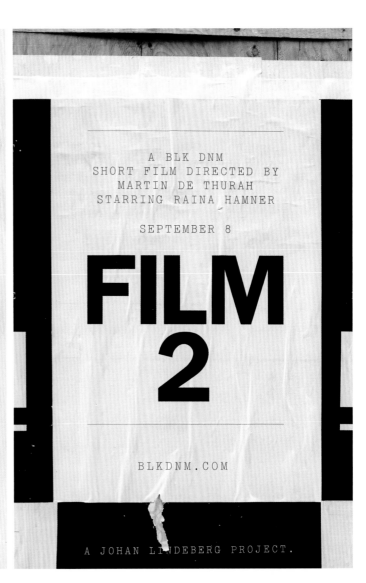

BLK DNM

Identity for the Museum of Modern Art (MoMA)

MoMA's identity has been a landmark of institutional branding since 1964, when the museum introduced its distinctive Franklin Gothic No.2 logotype designed by Ivan Chermayeff. In 2004 this logotype was redrawn in a new custom typeface, MoMA Gothic, created by Matthew Carter. Now MoMA has recast its identity, building on its familiar logotype to create a powerful and cohesive institutional voice. The new identity system expands on this logotype, making MoMA Gothic the principal font for all typography. More importantly, the system creates a complete methodology for the identity's application and handling across all platforms.

Client: Museum of Modern Art (MoMA)
Design Agency: Pentagram
Art Direction: Paula Scher/ Pentagram
Design: Paula Scher/ Pentagram, Julia Hoffman/ The Museum of Modern Art
Photography: Jim Brown
Fonts in Use: MoMA Gothic

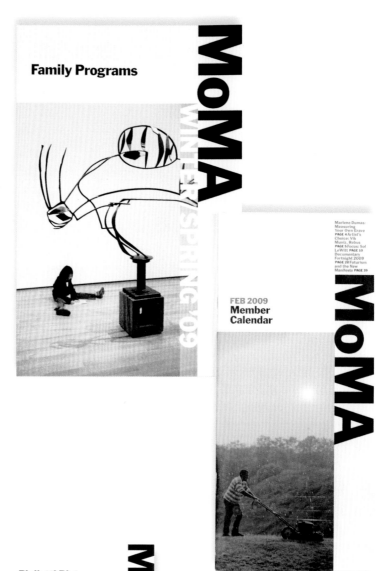

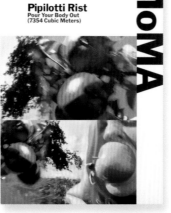

Identity for the Museum of Modern Art (MoMA)

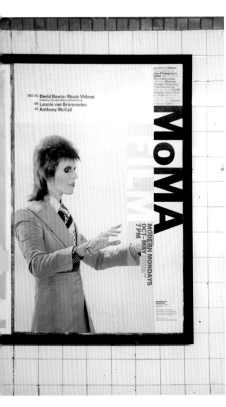

Identity for the Museum of Modern Art (MoMA)

Moderna Museet Stockholm

In February 2004, Moderna Museet triumphantly reopened its museum building after years of renovation caused by problems with mold. The museum's graphic profile was updated to coincide with the reopening.

Stockholm Design Lab, together with Henrik Nygren and Greger Ulf Nilson, created a comprehensive identity program for Moderna Museet. It included a new graphic identity and a design program for publications, merchandising and packaging. Two main requirements were applied when creating the new identity: to meet high standards of originality and aesthetics, and that all identity components should reflect the key values of Moderna Museet – excellence and access.

Client: Moderna Museet
Design Agency: Stockholm Design Lab
Creative Direction: Björn Kusoffsky
Art Direction: Henrik Nygren, Greger Ulf Nilson
Design: Stockholm Design Lab
Signature: Robert Rauschenberg
Photography: Brendan Austin, Emil Larsson
Project Partners: Henrik Nygren Design, Greger Ulf Nilson of SWE, TEA - Thomas Eriksson Architects, Marge Arkitekter
Fonts in Use: Gridnik MM/ Times MM

MINIMAL

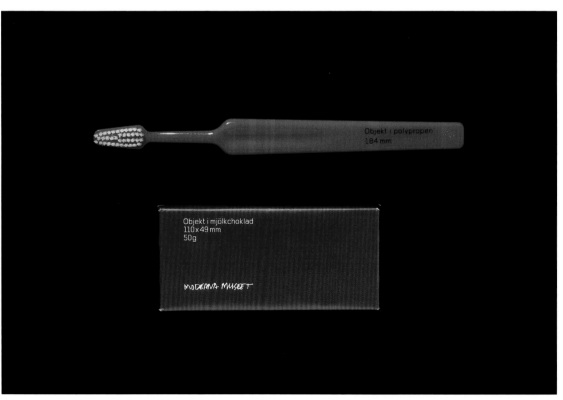

Moderna Museet Stockholm

ANDY WARHOL. FINAL WEEK

Other voices other room.
9 feb - 4 maj 2008

MODERNA MUSEET

Objekt i mjolkchoklad
110 x 49 mm
50g

MODERNA MUSEET

Objekt i m
110 x 49 r
50g

MODERNA

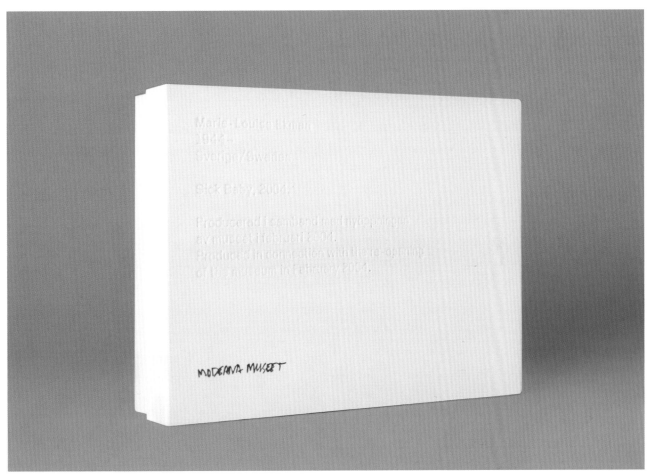

MODERNA MUSEET

Moderna Museet Stockholm

01:2 Framtid
The Future
1940–70

Öyvind Fahlström
Edward Kienholz
Yves Klein
Jackson Pollock
Robert Rauschenberg
Lena Svedberg m.fl.

MINIMAL

Moderna Museet Malmö

Moderna Museet Malmö

In 2008 it became clear that the Moderna Museet' Malmö would open as a subsidiary to Stockholm, in one of Sweden's most beautiful exhibition halls. It was time to re-fill the old electricity plant building with art. The mission to transform the building into a more appropriate museum went to the award-winning architect firm Tham & Videgård Arkitekter.

Stockholm Design Lab, together with Henrik Nygren and Greger Ulf Nilson, created a comprehensive identity program for Moderna Museet Malmö. It included a graphic identity and a design program for publications, merchandising and packaging. Two main requirements were applied when creating the new identity: to meet high standards of originality and aesthetics, and that all identity components should reflect the key values of Moderna Museet – excellence and access.

Client: Moderna Museet
Design Agency: Stockholm Design Lab
Creative Direction: Björn Kusoffsky
Art Direction: Henrik Nygren, Greger Ulf Nilson
Design: Stockholm Design Lab
Signature: Robert Rauschenberg
Photography: Åke E:son Lindman
Project Partners: Greger Ulf Nilson GunLab, Henrik Nygren Design, Tham & Videgård Arkitekter
Fonts in Use: Gridnik MM/ Times MM

Moderna Museet Malmö

INDEX

&Larry

▼*andlarry.com*

&Larry begins every project by putting the name of their client or creative partner before their own. This spirit of collaboration and mutual respect is reflected in the thinking that goes into each piece of work.

They believe that art and design shouldn't exist in separate vacuums. Be it commercial or experimental, &Larry always seeks to create works that are honest, functional and expressive beyond aesthetics.

The studio has adopted the Eames motto of "Take your pleasure seriously" and examples of this philosophy can be seen in a diverse body of work from posters and print campaigns to their series of Singapore-inspired art objects.

▲094-095

…, staat creative agency

▼*www.staatamsterdam.nl*

…, staat creative agency is an international creative agency based in Amsterdam, the Netherlands.

Set up in 2000, …, staat creative agency established itself as an independent world player. …, staat works with local heroes and global brands. The agency consists of original thinkers, who know no limits and deliver fully integrated branding, from strategy to concept to design. With passion, …, staat turns the everyday into the iconic, creating work that touches people.

▲140-141

84000 Communications (Stanley Wong)

▼*www.anothermountainman.com*

84000 Communications is specialized in graphic design, branding, cultural design, photography and creative multi-media communications. The founder of the company, Mr. Stanley Wong, has 30 years of experience in providing professional design and creative services in a wide array of design disciplines encompassing graphic design, advertising design, film & TV commercial production and fine arts. During his career, Mr. Wong has won more than 300 local and international awards including numerous Hong Kong Designers' Association Awards (Judge's Awards, Gold Awards), D&AD (Design & Advertising) Awards (UK), Hong Kong Institute of Professional Photographers (HKIPP) Annual Awards and Media Asian Awards. In 2004, Mr. Stanley Wong was inducted into the Alliance Graphique Internationale (AGI), the world's most prestigious institution which is comprised of worldwide leading graphic designers and artists. Also known as "anothermountainman", Mr. Wong is deeply involved and well known in the art scene, with active participation in local and overseas cultural, fine arts and photography exhibitions.

▲052-053

A

Alex Dalmau

▼*alexdalmau.com*

Alex Dalmau is an art director based in Barcelona. He specializes in graphic design, branding and corporate identity. After graduating from Image and Design School (IDEP), he worked at various advertising agencies and design studios like Animal-BCN, Larsson-Duprez, and Creatica and began working as a freelancer in 2011. He has worked for clients such as Progess, Mandarin Oriental Barcelona, Carolina Herrera 212, Adidas, Ricola, Font Vella, Reig Capital and others.

▲160-161

Alexandra Kuznetsova

▼*www.behance.net/alexku*

Alexandra Kuznetsova is an artist and graphic designer.

He lives and works in Moscow (Russia). He is 32 years old and more than those years he works in graphic design. His specialization is editorial design but he is also occupied with brand design, type and typography. For the last two years he has been a lecturer at the British Higher School of Art and Design (Moscow). Since 2010 he has been a member of Art Directors Club Russia.

He loves graphic design, but the most interesting thing for him is contemporary art. He participates in exhibitions with installation works, animation and video art.

▲150-151

All the Way to Paris

▼*allthewaytoparis.com*

ATWTP is a Danish-Swedish graphic design studio based in Copenhagen. Founded in 2004 by Tanja Vibe and Petra Olsson Gendt, they work conceptually with visual communication in small and large scale. Elin Kinning joined ATWTP in 2006 and Matilde Rasmussen joined in 2008. They're currently a team of six people.

▲133

Alt Group

▼*www.altgroup.net*

Alt Group is a multidisciplinary design company based in Auckland, New Zealand. Founded in 2000 by Ben Corban and Dean Poole, the company has a core team of 20 people with a rich diversity of design, business backgrounds and experience working in brand strategy, communication design, interactive design and new product development. The company has been recognized in numerous international awards such as ADC, AIGA, AGDA, Cannes Lions, The One Show, Red Dot, TDC and Webby Awards.

▲206-207, 208-209

Amélie Wagner

▼*www.ameliewagner.fr*

Amélie Wagner is a French graphic designer, who likes mixing design with illustration, photography, sculpture, and research. She creates attractive end results without forgetting

the theme or message.

She likes to work on graphic projects and plastic projects, and thinks the two areas correspond well.

▲080-081

Anagrama

▼*anagrama.com*

Anagrama is a specialized brand development and positioning agency providing creative solutions for any type of projects. Besides their history and experience with brand development, they are also experts in the design and development of objects, spaces and multimedia projects. They create the perfect balance between acting as a design boutique that focuses on the development of creative pieces and paying attention to the smallest of details, and a business consultancy providing solutions based on the analysis of tangible data to generate the best fit of applications. Their services reach all of the branding spectrum from strategic consulting to fine tuning brand objectives for the company to logotype, peripherals and illustration design.

▲028-029, 038-041, 056

Andrés Requena

▼*www.andresrequena.es*

Andrés Requena is from Viladecans (Barcelona, Spain.) He believes in the shape's synthesis as a way of explicit/direct communication, avoiding needless visual elements. He always tries to add objectivity to his work by facing the lack of REAL information and dissembled advertising that people are submitted to every day.

▲157

Apartment One

▼*aptone.com*

Apartment One is an award winning creative agency based in Brooklyn, NY that works thoughtfully and intimately with today's leading companies, organizations and individuals to give voice to the truth, presence and power of their brands. Founded in 2005 by Liza Lowinger and Spencer Bagley, Apartment One offers a customized approach to every client and project, digging deep to discover, identify and reveal the core truths that make each brand authentic, distinctive and ownable. Their innovative and creative work has generated numerous industry accolades and awards including the prestigious AIGA 365:31 Annual Design Award, HOW International Design Awards, Print Creativity & Commerce Awards, Print Regional Annual Design Awards and inclusion in numerous books and international publications.

▲128-129

Asylum

▼*www.theasylum.com.sg*

Asylum is defined as a creative company that is comprised of a design studio, a retail store, workshop and a record label. Since its inception in 1999, they have worked on cross disciplinary projects that includes interactive design, product development, environmental & interior design, packaging, apparel design, branding and graphic design.

e-Types

▼*www.e-types.com*

e-Types is a strategic brand and design agency that moves companies and organizations forward through identity. Brand leadership is characterized by the clear signals of an organization permeated by a strong sense of identity and purpose. e-Types illuminates corporate ideas. Through brand strategy and graphic design embedded in big ideas, they nurture enthusiasm, increase sales and enhance leadership.

▲218-219

Face

▼*www.designbyface.com*

Founded in 2006, Face is an intelligence-driven super modernist design studio, based in Monterrey, Mexico, whose work range includes design solutions, advertising, editorial projects and custom publishing, corporate identity and brand development. Face applies a global perspective to its projects and offers specific, applicable creative answers to premium brands in various areas. They directly approach each brand to know them integrally in order to build them customized solutions based on their unique needs. Their craft is firmly rooted on the networking of talent, which not only relies on their capacity to summon, but also on their ability to orchestrate the most capable creative minds around. Through this personalized process, and based on their expertise & know-how, their clients achieve an outstanding and desirable company.

▲198

FEB Design

▼*www.feb-design.com*

FEB Design is a design collective based in Oporto Portugal, which has been developing multidisciplinary projects since 2009 and specializes in corporate identity, branding, signage systems, websites, packaging, exhibition and book design.

▲084-085, 204-205

Figtree

▼*www.figtreenetwork.com*

Figtree is an independent brand consultancy that helps a wide range of organizations achieve their potential by developing clear brand strategies, strong personalities and engaging experiences. A diverse and international group of strategists, creatives, thinkers and doers, they're here to define and develop standout brands that connect with customers and make an impact in the market.

▲146-147

Frankenstein Studio

▼*www.frankenstein.se*

Frankenstein is a creative studio building brand identities and their emotional values through visible and tangible communication. The studio work is cross disciplinary to realize this vision, implementing creative direction, design strategy, product design, interior design and advertising.

▲114-115

Glasfurd & Walker

▼*glasfurdandwalker.com*

Glasfurd & Walker offer cross-disciplinary, conceptual services, innovative brand communication and design solutions.

The studio applies creative thinking and understanding of design to develop thought-provoking solutions to address commercial needs. The team works hard to build partnerships with their clients to understand their communication challenges.

During the course of the project the studio spends time meticulously crafting the detail and nuance while keeping an eye on the bigger picture to deliver a product that is interesting and relevant. The team is driven by a passion and commitment to design excellence.

▲048-049, 060-061

H

H55

▼*www.h55studio.com*

Hanson Ho is an award winning Creative Director who works under the studio name of H55, which he founded in 1999. Since then, Hanson has created numerous visual identities, brand applications, and publications which have represented Singapore on an international level.

Featured by the Sunday Times as one of the top Graphic Designers in Singapore, Hanson has received recognition and awards from some of the most prestigious international design competitions for his works, including the British D&AD, New York Type Directors Club, New York One Show Design, Creative Circle Awards, Tokyo Type Directors Club, and the New York Art Directors Club.

▲054-055

Hey

▼*heystudio.es*

Hey is a multidisciplinary design studio based in Barcelona, Spain, specializing in brand management and editorial design, packaging and interactive design. They share the profound conviction that good design means combining content, functionality, graphic expression and strategy. As a result, they offer their clients a personal service based on mutual understanding and trust, working to innovate from rationality and directing advice to meet actual needs.

▲062-063

HORT

▼*hort.de*

HORT began its inhabitance back in 1994, under the previous stage name of EIKES GRAFISCHER HORT. Who the hell is Eike?

Eike is the creator of HORT. HORT - a direct translation of the studio's mission. A creative playground. A place where "work and play" can be said in the same sentence. An unconventional working environment. Once a household name in the music industry. Now, a multi-disciplinary creative hub. Not just a studio space, but an institution devoted to making ideas come to life. A place to learn, a place to grow, and a place that is still growing. Not a client execution tool. HORT has been known to draw inspiration from things other than design.

▲126-127

I

I LIKE BIRDS

▼*www.ilikebirds.de*

I LIKE BIRDS is a studio located in the Speicherstadt in the port of Hamburg where they work on turning designs into creations. They take great pleasure in experimenting with various mediums to develop customized and interesting solutions. Their activities focus on transforming numerous types of information into a visual language which conveys the content in a more fluid and effective manner. They put a lot of time and effort into creating a wide range of print products, including posters, books, illustrations, corporate identities and other visual works for cultural and public purposes.

To maximize their output, they are also very happy to work on their own projects to try out new methods and approaches to benefit their day-to-day work, which includes creating fonts, installations, posters, textiles and other crafts produced and published in limited editions.

▲164-165

Ideas Factory

▼*www.ideasfactory.co.uk*

Ideas Factory is a multi-disciplinary graphic design studio with over 25 years experience in building brands and creating acclaimed design.

Their work involves identity design, printed matter, digital design, art direction and advertising.

They help their clients understand how they can develop and transform their business by increasing their brand's value. Creating impactful design crafted with their trademark attention to detail and concept led approaches are key to their success.

▲212-213

Interbrand

▼*www.interbrand.com*

Interbrand started in 1974 when the world still thought of brands as just another word for logo. Since then, they have helped change brands into valuable business assets. In fact, they believe brands can change the world. And they believe the only way to do this is to have an idea. Equal parts logic and magic. The product of discovery, truth, bravery and imagination. The undeniable and unbroken thread that connects everything you create, every decision you make, every action you take. Ideas are their obsession. In their studios in Sydney and Melbourne, it's this obsession that makes them stand apart, and it underpins the work they create for their clients, their businesses and brands.

▲072-073, 096-097

IYA Studio

▼iyastudio.co.uk

IYA is an independent creative studio in London working across a broad spectrum of projects covering commercial interiors, digital and graphics. With clients such as Folk, Hudson, Oliver Spencer and Exposure, they believe a collaborative process is the best way to create well crafted, memorable design from concept to execution. They are as passionate about embracing new tech and materials for both their digital and spatial projects as they are about design and their ever expanding network of expert partners enables them to push their creativity without constraint. Their experience and knowledge of working on projects large and small means they're very much open for new challenges whatever the size or budget. For them they truly believe the creative partnership is the key to a successful outcome.

▲124-125, 200-201

J

Jaemin Lee

▼leejaemin.net

Jaemin Lee has been working as an art director at studio fnt which he found in 2006. Lee is a lecturer at Seoul National University, Seoul Women's University and Kaywon School of Art & Design, and has special lectures at the University of Seoul, Seoul Women's University, Hongik University and Seoul National University. He also gave a lecture at CA conference and Sangsangmadang forum in Seoul. Lee has participated in many exhibitions including TYPOJANCHI 2011: International Typography Biennale, Design Korea 2010, Connected Project in Graphic Design Festival Breda, Wired Book and etc. Lee was the winner of 2010 Reddot Design Award and Web Award Korea. His works and interviews were featured in many publications such as Typography Workshop 6, Design magazine, g: magazine, CA magazine and so on.

▲170-171

Jiwon Kim

▼www.thejiwonkim.com

Originally from Seoul, South Korea, Jiwon Kim received her BFA in Graphic Design at School of Visual Arts. While attending school, she was profiled in the G.D USA Magazine "Students to Watch" as one of the 14 talented graphic design students in the U.S. She received Gold, Silver, and Bronze awards for Art Directors Club 90th Annual Award and Typographic Excellence certificates for logo design for Type director's club 31 and 32. She was also announced an Adobe Design Achievement Awards (ADAA) finalist in 2011 and has displayed her work in Taipei and L.A. In addition, she has been featured in numerous magazines, including

Communication Arts Typography 2011, TDC 31 and 32, ADC 90th Annual, How promotion Annual design 2010, CMYK#48, Graphics New Talent Annual 2011.

▲180-181

Johanna Bonnevier

▼www.johannabonnevier.com

Johanna Bonnevier is a Swedish art director, graphic designer and illustrator based in East London. She mainly works with architecture, culture and fashion based projects, ranging from both small and large scale print jobs to film credits and installations, and some of her clients has been Fashion East, b store, Embassy of Sweden, 42 architects, Lulu & Co, The Bartlett School of Architecture, UCL amongst others. She was educated at Central Saint Martins and Camberwell College of Art and Design, and has since graduating both been freelancing and working full-time whilst running her own practice.

▲118-119

K

Kentlyons

▼www.kentlyons.com

They are a design agency, with work spanning branding, digital, print, advertising, strategy and environmental design.

Formed in 2003, KentLyons is a team of designers and developers based in London. They're focused on creating communications that are simultaneously beautiful and useful. Their work wins awards, is highly effective, and moves people. Their team is made up of Design, Visual Communications, Arts and Computer Science experts. They can produce effortlessly elegant books, or intuitive iPad reading experiences with the same ease as well as creating clear, compelling ideas, and communicating them with style, simplicity and passion.

▲026-027

Kevin Cantrell

▼www.kevincantrell.com

Although he currently call Utah his home, he has lived in Germany, South Africa, Brazil and New York. These experiences have helped him understand brand ethnographic influences. His approach is guided by the same process: to strategically and elegantly communicate a story that resonates with the audience.

He is currently an art director at Hint Creative in SLC.

▲030-031, 046-047

kissmiklos (Miklos Kiss)

▼kissmiklos.com

Designer and visual artist. Currently architecture, design and graphic design are his work fields. There is an outstanding aesthetic quality and strong artistic approach characterizing his implementation of work.

▲070-071, 104-107

Kurppa Hosk

▼www.kurppahosk.com

Kurppa Hosk is an interdisciplinary brand and design consultancy creating attraction. They offer expertise within various disciplines such as brand and design strategy, corporate identity, art direction, storytelling, retail design, digital design and technology, packaging design and product design. By attraction they mean putting as much love, innovation and craftsmanship as possible into their work.

Besides having some of Sweden's most talented and renowned creatives in-house they have an extensive international network of designers and innovators to fulfill their inter-disciplinary+attraction mission.

▲057

L

La Tigre

▼www.latigre.net

La Tigre is an independent media studio in Milan, founded and directed by the designers Margherita Paleari, Walter Molteni and Luisa Milani. Since its opening in 2009, La Tigre takes on a wide variety of projects of different types, such as web, printing, branding, editing and illustrating, always exploring original and alternative solutions.

Their graphic language is precise, direct, and driven by the use of basic elements like color, geometry and typography. Thanks to their union with creative and semantic research, they produce highly communicative visual systems with strong identities.

▲042-043

lg2boutique

▼lg2boutique.com

lg2boutique, is the branding atelier within lg2. They specialize in communications and advertising design, brand strategy, packaging, print production and product design. Founded in 2006, lg2boutique quickly established itself as an industry leader by collaborating closely with each of their clients to create visually compelling, strategically insightful work. As a result, in partnership with clients like Agropur, Bell, Boris, Evenko, Telefilm Canada and Maison Orphée, they have already become one of the most award-winning design agencies in the country.

▲210-211

M

MAGA - atelier

▼www.maga-atelier.com

José Mendes, Luís Alvoeiro and Carlos Guerreiro were long time colleagues who, following an old dream, set up their own practice in 2009. MAGA is a design studio in Lisbon (Chiado), which develops tailored solutions for the needs and ambitions of its clients. It is not a supplier, but rather a partner in the projects it takes. It is driven by its love of

Design. It constantly looks for new solutions that give its projects a unique identity.
▲188-189

Magpie Studio

▼*magpie-studio.com*

There is a simple approach: listen to the clients; understand their audience; solve their problems.

They've learnt that it's easier to make yourself understood when you speak in black and white. It helps to move beyond the grey areas and deliver a message loud and clear (or quiet and clear, if the brief requires).

But there's more to it than that. They're avid collectors of all things visual. They're passionate about creative color – the bright idea that catches the eye, connects with an audience and makes a message memorable.

▲018-019

Manifiesto Futura

▼*mfutura.mx*

Manifiesto Futura, an independent design studio based in Mexico, was founded in 2008. Nowadays they've grown and expanded their services, and have become a multidisciplinary firm, offering a variety of services and solutions for diverse customers. Their goal is to make the best of Mexican design, to chance the shapes. Narratives are created through clear messages and smart incentives. They value experimentation, the reformation of messages, and smart incentives. They believe in the atypical, and in the principle that says that form follows function. They celebrate clear messages and intelligent content.

▲082-083

Marnich Associates

▼*www.marnich.com*

Marnich is a design and communication consultancy based in Barcelona.

They believe in simplicity and clarity. Their clients range from small restaurants, independent publishers and music festivals to large corporations, banks and museums. Their work has been recognized with many design awards and has also appeared in design publications around the globe.

▲074-075

Mash Creative

▼*www.mashcreative.co.uk*

Mash Creative is an independent design studio based in East London/Essex. They work on creative projects that include identity & branding, print media and web design. In a short space of time they have acquired a reputation for producing innovative and effective graphic design that is engaging, clear and relevant. They don't believe in just one approach, which is why their work is always unique - producing relevant and successful solutions which add value to their clients' brands.

▲192-193, 194-195

Matt Maurer

▼*www.mattmaurer.co.uk*

He is a designer who likes to make sure

that there is is a unique idea at the heart of everything he does. He believes that a unique idea will help create an effective piece of communication – be it creating awareness, selling, attracting more visitors or educating.

▲044-045

MENOSUNOCEROUNO

▼*www.menosunocerouno.com*

MENOSUNOCEROUNO is an advertising agency, a branding boutique, an editorial house, and a digital agency designed as a "one stop shop". Their Agency structure enables them to speak four languages: Business, Strategy, Creativity and Design.

They translate their clients' business strategy into mobilizing communication strategies. They create simple and powerful stories connecting people with brands and brands with people.

Brands should always smell, taste, feel, sound, look, speak and behave in a way that becomes unforgettable. Since 2001 the creative work of MENOSUNOCEROUNO is recognized for its powerful simplicity and surgical aesthetic.

▲132

Micha Weidmann Studio

▼*michaweidmannstudio.com*

Micha Weidmann Studio is an art direction and design studio based in London helping creators of high-end products to build their brands. They assist publishers and art galleries with their publications, exhibitions and online appearances.

The studio's creative approach is based on Micha Weidmann's background in Swiss design and art direction defined through working with brands such as Prada, The Tate Modern and Zaha Hadid.

▲012-013

MICHAELHANSENWORK

▼*michaelhansenwork.dk*

Michael Hansen is a student of visual communication at School of Design, The Royal Danish Academy of Fine Arts. He works primarily with conceptual ideas that explore the world of graphic design. He also works with fashion photography and visual identity design.

▲066-067

Mind Design

▼*www.minddesign.co.uk*

Mind Design is a London-based independent graphic design studio founded by Holger Jacobs in 1999 after graduating from the Royal College of Art. The studio specializes in the development of visual identities and has worked for a wide range of clients in different sectors.

▲130-131, 182-185

moodley brand identity

▼*www.moodley.at*

moodley brand identity is an owner-led, award-winning strategic design agency with offices in Vienna and Graz. Since 1999 moodley has worked together with its customers to develop corporate and product brands which live,

breathe and grow. moodley believes that the key contribution is to analyze complex requirements and develop simple, smart solutions with emotional appeal – whether corporate start-up, product launch or brand positioning. The team currently consists of more than 40 employees.

▲068-069, 076-079, 086-087

Morey Talmor

▼*www.moreytalmor.com*

Morey Talmor is a graphic designer from Tel Aviv, Israel, currently living and working in Brooklyn, New York.

His work includes various aspects of design for printed media, such as: editorial design, identities, packaging design and illustration.

He graduated from Shenkar College of Engineering and Design in 2011 with a B.D in Visual Communications.

▲032-033, 090-091

Mother Design

▼*motherdesign.com*

Mother Design is a design and branding group within Mother New York. They create fully integrated brand communications that are anchored in strategy, culture and design. During their seven years experience, they've made identity systems, books, billboards, apps, films, websites, packages, whiskey, political t-shirts, environments and more.

▲016-017, 022-023

N

Nakano Design Office

▼*nakano-design.com*

Nakano Design Office is a design firm which mainly works on graphic design.

They seek possibilities in functional design by understanding the core values of the objects. They would like to continue to create artwork for a long time.

▲110-111

Network Osaka

▼*www.networkosaka.com*

Network Osaka is an "artist pretending to be a designer" (what he self-proclaimed). With the presentation, style, and workload of a full-on design studio, he creates strikingly bold and intimidatingly intelligent, yet beautifully simplistic, imagery. He has a great sense of when and how to use heavy, solid bodies of color. Derek Kim, as he is also known, is a Parsons graduate with a BFA in communication, carrying a respectable client list which holds such names as Wieden+Kennedy, Nike, Esquire, and YWFT. Recently, he was awarded both the Platinum and Gold prizes in the 2011 Graphics Poster Annual. Additionally, he's done innovative Braille type work, skate deck designs, concert posters, and a whole cadre of other side projects.

▲158-159

NIGN Company Limited

▼*www.nign.co.jp*

Kenichiro Ohara Art Director/ Graphic Designer, NIGN Company Limited.

Kenichiro Ohara was born in Hyogo in 1973. After graduating from an industrial high school, Kenichiro has self-taught the discipline of design throughout a wide range of professional careers. In 2000, Kenichiro became a freelance designer and in 2006, he founded his own design firm NIGN. NIGN has been a gateway to an extensive field of design services, including CI, branding, book design, fashion, and packaging. He is also a member of Tokyo Type Directors Club and Japan Graphic Designers Association.

▲050-051

O

Oat

▼*www.oatcreative.com*

Founded in 2008, Oat is a design studio focused on the value of creating a strong brand image. They capture the essence of a consumer experience through art direction, graphic design, photography, illustration and web technology. It is a studio where staying small keeps them efficient and intimate with every project.

The creative process is a winding, often magical, sometimes difficult and always time-consuming endeavor. With each project, the execution of a unique idea is an opportunity to introduce something new to the world.

▲134-135

P

Pentagram

▼*www.pentagram.com*

Pentagram is the world's largest independent design consultancy. The firm is owned and run by 19 partners, a group of friends who are all leaders in their individual creative fields.

They work in London, New York, San Francisco, Berlin and Austin. They design everything: architecture, interiors, products, identities, publications, posters, books, exhibitions, websites, and digital installations.

Each of their clients works directly with one or more of our partners. This reflects their conviction that great design cannot happen without passion, intelligence, and personal commitment, which is demonstrated by a portfolio of work that spans five decades.

▲186-187, 226-227

Present Perfect

▼*www.presentperfect.com*

Present Perfect is a London based design practice formed in 2011 by Ivan Markovic and Povilas Utovka. They work on a broad range of projects, focusing on graphic design, art direction and type design. Their clients include individuals, businesses and cultural organizations.

▲156

R

Raum Mannheim

▼*hraum-mannheim.com*

Raum Mannheim is an office for visual communication. They develop exceptional images and identities. They design and implement the visual presence for their clients through texts, graphics, illustrations, and photographs. They love the challenge of understanding and structuring complex subjects and then transcribing them precisely into various media forms. They think comprehensively, but quality for them lies in details. It is not the size of a project that matters, but rather the specific tasks involved and the individual form it takes on – from an unusual idea to an intriguing concept to a distinctive aesthetic expression. These are the projects that excite their imagination and challenge their abilities. The courage their clients show through willingness to move in unknown territories and use of innovative forms of communication is rewarded with a unique and unmistakable corporate design. They are also continually extending their own design spectrum through their art projects.

They want to cross borders – the borders of perception, the usual, the expected. They want to make a mark in the increasingly standardized world of images.

▲024-025

Reynolds and Reyner

▼*reynoldsandreyner.com*

In Reynolds and Reyner they truly believe in a power of design. It's not about making modern and high quality design, it's an approach to process, of which the result will serve as the basis for communications between brand and consumers.

Three main principles: listen to the client; understand his audience; make people believe.

▲102-103

S

Stockholm Design Lab

▼*www.stockholmdesignlab.se*

Since 1998 SDL has helped over 500 brands to successfully stand out by strengthening the brand's equity. They operate in all kind of industries from airlines, spirits, museums, fashion, hotels, and consumer goods to retail environments and pharmacies both in Sweden and overseas. Their philosophy is rooted in Scandinavian tradition based on the fundamental ideas of simplicity, clarity, openness and innovation. Their approach is holistic and their areas of expertise are insights, brand strategy, graphic design, retail design, digital design and communication platforms. SDL is the most awarded design agency in Scandinavia and has been exhibited around the world.

▲100-101, 228-231

Studio Egregius

▼*studio-egregius.com*

Studio Egregius is a multidisciplinary design studio, doodling while kerning, painting while writing, snap-shooting while die-cutting, coding while rendering, googling while daydreaming, self-caffeinating while brainstorming, working hard while keeping sane. Studio Egregius was founded in 2009, by Le Huy Anh and Nguyen Quang Trung. They are concept-based and creative-led.

They listen, listen, research, research, research, brainstorm, research, create, listen, refine, listen more, refine some more, until the work is done. They are hungry for success and won't settle for less.

▲144-145

Studio Laucke Siebein

▼*www.studio-laucke-siebein.com*

Studio Laucke Siebein is a design studio based in Amsterdam and Berlin. Its focus is on creative strategy, dynamic identities, graphic, book and web design within the scope of cultural and commercial projects.

Dirk Laucke and Johanna Siebein has been awarded, amongst others, the Art Directors Club NY, The European Design Award, The Best Dutch Books, The Dutch Design Award and the Dutch Corporate Identity Award. Their work has been presented in large number of magazines and books.

▲172-173

Studio Lin

▼*www.studiolin.org*

Studio Lin is the graphic design practice of Alex Lin. Their work process is founded on a desire to explore new territory through challenging collaborations with creative visionaries in the fields of architecture, industrial design, art and fashion. By combining the studio's analytical rigor with strong input from external forces, the resulting design is exponentially enhanced: 1 + 1 =3. This formula also permits a fluid aesthetic to prevail. Behind every Studio Lin design is a highly defined rationale but not a singular style. The common denominator is a fresh, modern sensibility that eschews the overtly trendy in favor of lasting impact.

In 2005 Alex was named an Art Director's Club Young Gun, in 2006 he was in STEP magazine's field guide for emerging designers, and in 2009 he was honored as an Avant Guardian by Surface Magazine. In 2007 his Mies face artwork created at 2x4 became part of the permanent collection at the Museum of Modern Art.

▲199

StudioMakgill

▼*www.studiomakgill.com*

StudioMakgill is a Brighton-based design studio, founded in 2007 by Hamish Makgill. They create simple, beautiful, intuitive designs that help their clients connect with the audience.

Their focus is on the creation of brand identities that work as well in print as they do on screen. They work for a range of clients within a variety of sectors, and they're as comfortable creating an identity for a range of cosmetics as they are a look and feel for a successful tapas restaurant in north London. They're passionate about good design and revel in the details of a project. They look to inspire their clients whilst having a lasting effect on their business.

Sunday Morning

▼ *www.sundaymorningny.com*

Sunday Morning is a Graphic Design studio located in New York City, focused on design platforms for brands, institutions & individuals

T

Taku Satoh Design inc.

▼ *www.tsdo.jp*

Established in 1984, they specialize in graphic design, commercial design, and branding and planning for exhibitions, books, and other projects. They are also involved in the planning of and art direction for TV programs on a children's educational channel.

Thorleifur Gunnar Gíslason

▼ *www.thorleifur.is*

Having recently graduated from the Icelandic Academy of the Arts, Thorleifur now works as a graphic designer for Jónsson & Le'macks advertising agency in Reykjavík as well as being a member of the multidisciplinary design crew Wolfgang.

Triboro

▼ *triborodesign.com*

Triboro is the Brooklyn based design team of David Heasty and Stefanie Weigler. The studio's client base ranges from innovative start-ups to established international brands. Recent projects include branding the fashion labels BLK DNM and William Rast, art directing the GQ Style Manual, illustrating a campaign for Stella Artois, designing albums for Blonde Redhead as well as materials for MoMA and the Dia Art Foundation. In addition to client work, Triboro pursues self-initiated experiments such as their One-Color Subway Map and Triboro Leftovers. David & Stefanie have received numerous industry awards including being named Art Directors Club Young Guns.

Tsto

▼ *www.tsto.org*

Tsto is a creative consultancy founded by six designers. They are graphic design professionals specialized in coming up with ideas and visualizing them. Their approach is thorough and hands-on. They tackle an assignment by first taking it apart to its bare essentials, and then building it in a new way that best serves the client. This design philosophy let them go deeper than the surface, to the essence of each case. They also work with other proven professionals in whatever media the work requires. Instead of competing with other creatives or agencies, they see them as possible collaborators for best serving each case.

Tsto was founded by Johannes Ekholm, Jonatan Eriksson, Inka Järvinen, Matti Kunttu, Jaakko Pietiläinen and Antti Uotila.

TYMOTE

▼ *tymote.jp*

A creative team that centers around graphic design and produces art works for video pictures, computer graphics, music, interface designing, web designing, and etc.

The members are Q Asaba, Kent Iitaka, Rei Ishii, Kota Iguchi, Akiou Kato, Satoshi Murai, Hitoshi Morita and Takahiro Yamaguchi.

To seek high level work, ideas, and project planning, they break down and reconstruct the project by analyzing it from multiple perspectives.

Ward Heirwegh

▼ *www.wardheirwegh.com*

Ward Heirwegh (1982) graduated in 2007 as a master in typography at the Sint Lucas academy in Ghent, Belgium. In 2009 he started his independent practice as a graphic designer and art director, expressing an interest in editorial design. Next to his studio he also founded a research-based, ephemeral platform for artist publications called Sleeperhold Publications. So far SHP has released a photobook, a silkscreen poster set, a deck of gaming cards, a collection of short stories and several vinyl records. Next to these outputs Ward is also giving lectures about his design and research work.

Y

Yooin Cho

▼ *yooincho.com*

Born in Seoul, South Korea. Yooin Cho is a graphic designer based in New York City, graduated with BFA Graphic Design at the School of Visual Arts. Focusing on identity, environmental graphics, along with explorations in digital media, her work has been published in CMYK, HOW Magazine, and Graphis in addition to winning Clio, International Design Award and Brand New Award Annuals.

YOUMAAN

▼ *www.youmaan.com*

YOUMAAN is the pseudonym of Mark Niemeijer, a twenty-one year old graphic design student and independent graphic designer from the Netherlands.

Ever since he was a child he had been interested in art and eventually this affection led him to graphic design. What moves him in visual communication and plays the leading in carrying out design is to help people express themselves and impress others.

ACKNOWLEDGEMENTS

We would like to acknowledge our gratitude to the artists and designers for their generous contributions of images, ideas and concepts. We are very grateful to many other people whose names do not appear on the credits but who provided assistance and support. Thanks also go to people who have worked hard on the book and put ungrudging efforts into it. Our editorial team includes editor Yvonne Syan Yi and book designer Deng Liling, to whom we are truly grateful. Without you all, the creation and ongoing development of this book would not have been possible. Thank you for sharing your innovation and creativity with all our readers.

ACKNOWLEDGEMENTS